There is no silver bullet to solve ecological problems, nor any single answer to how people should live — and yet, we must seek new ways to think and act in light of environmental challenges. This is the issue at stake for design today.

Design has historically been employed in service to expanding industrial production and consumer culture — perhaps it is no wonder that design has often been seen as part of the problem within sustainability discourse. On the defensive, much has been done to reposition design as part of the solution, for example, through design roles in reforming production and reducing consumption. Sustainability, however, requires fundamentally rethinking the organization of everyday life in terms such as ecological complexity, social responsibility and risky futures. A role for design in this is to question the status quo, to critically reframe the issues at hand by materializing alternatives within the here and now. Such a role for design increases its agency within social processes, in which the materials and methods of design mobilize critical reflection and influence public discourse.

Critical approaches are concerned with finding problems and formulating questions within design and within society. Design, amended as 'critical', may query production and consumption, social structures and norms. Critical practices of design do not produce the traditional 'objects' of design, intended to be built or lived in, industrially produced or mass-consumed. As in 'paper architecture', for example, the object might be a conceptual space, in which the status quo may be materialized, debated and reimagined. Such practices are deeply rooted in design skills,

Introduction

processes and materiality — conceptual spaces must be carefully crafted to bring alternatives and futures to life. To make these matter within the present, arenas for critical discourse and cultural imaginaries must be designed. This might sound like art, activism or sci-fi (or, at least, not design as it has been institutionalized in museums, magazines and shops) though a geneology of precedents may be traced through avant-garde and counter-design movements. Such practices practices provide vivid reformulations — and urgently needed visions — of what design could be and what society could look like.

'Switch!' is an attempt to create a space for reflecting upon the current status and strategies within design discourse concerning sustainability and environmentalism. Evading design genres of greenwashing and eco-horror, future utopias and dystopias, we have been attempting to raise more fundamental questions. We ask, for example, how does design mediate people's access to nature and control over resources? What kinds of futures — or who's — do we assume, desire and determine by design? How are environmental experiences, risks and values made visible in everyday life? In our work, we investigate design as giving form to alternative and future ways of everyday life. Design becomes an arena for engaging others in the ecological and political dimensions of sustainable development.

We locate critical reflection on such questions within design — as practice-based research that produces criticism not only of, but through, design. In this, we are also grappling with a range of further questions material to design.

How can processes of design making, prototyping and exhibiting become arenas for debating sustainability? What kinds of concepts and methods do we bring to sustainability as designers, and how do we learn from and engage with other disciplines? In what ways can we combine critique and proposition, theory and practice, within design? This book embodies our inquiry as the story of Switch!, a design research program carried out since 2008 by an international team of designers, artists, architects, computer and social scientists at the Interactive Institute in Sweden.

Switch! queries energy consumption in everyday life. We investigate energy within the multiple technical, material and social systems — or ecologies — that comprise everyday life. Through the intervention of designs that disrupt existing — and introduce new — values within particular sites and situations, our aim is to influence the perception of energy within a given ecology. Design includes concepts, visualizations, scenarios and prototypes, at the scale of products, architecture and urbanism. These become vehicles for critical reflection in public forums, contexts of consumption and among stakeholders in design, planning and policy-making. In this way, we explore the agency of design in crafting and staging alternatives within everyday life, consumer culture and environmental discourse.

Through a series of collaborative and experimental processes, Switch! has been built up out of six projects:

Energy Futures

Ramia Mazé, Aude Messager,
Thomas Thwaites, Basar Önal

Based on energy forecasts and social trends drawn from futures studies, 'Energy Futures' revisits familiar urban and domestic artifacts in light of potentially emerging behaviors, beliefs and politics. Countering both the incremental reforms of user-centered design and the utopias and dystopias of visionary architecture, the project investigates the design of transitions between the familiar now and extreme futures. The project takes the form of fictional scenarios in which a series of redesigned artifacts (fore)tell stories of transformed lifestyles and urban life. Presented as a (super)fictive reality, Energy Futures operates as a platform for hosting a debate with stakeholders about probable and preferred futures of electricity consumption.

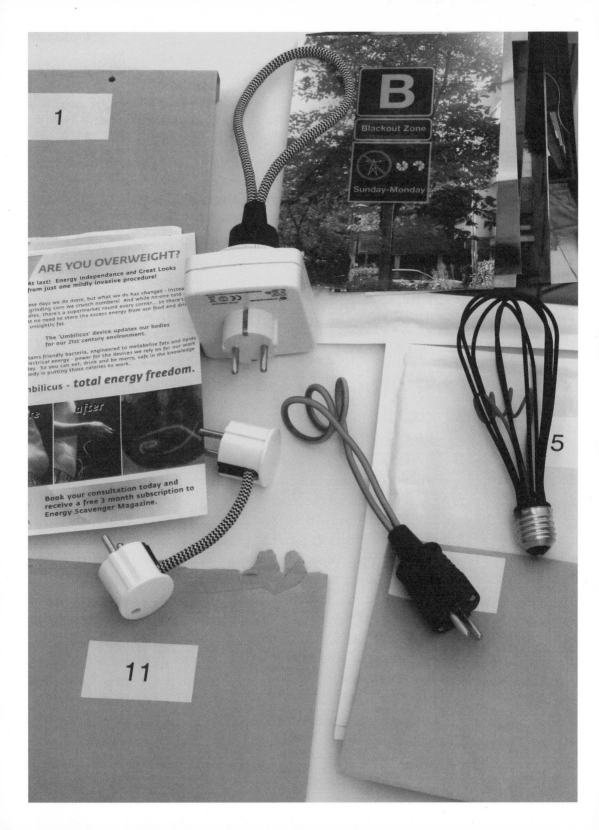

1

B
Blackout Zone
Sunday-Monday

ARE YOU OVERWEIGHT?

At last! Energy Independance and Great Looks from just one mildly invasive procedure!

ese days we do more, but what we do has changed - instea grinding corn we crunch numbers! And while no-one told dies, there's a supermarket round every corner... so there's st no need to store the excess energy from our food and dri unsightly fat.

The 'Umbilicus' device updates our bodies for our 21st century environment.

tains friendly bacteria, engineered to metabolise fats and lipids lectrical energy - power for the devices we rely on for our work ay. So you can eat, drink and be merry, safe in the knowledge ody is putting those calories to work.

mbilicus - total energy freedom.

e   after

Book your consultation today and receive a free 3 month subscription to Energy Scavenger Magazine.

5

11

Projecting futures of energy use

Energy Futures explores alternative methods for projecting possible futures. In part, this developed as a reaction to the incremental change typically promoted by user-centered design approaches to sustainability, which tend to perpetuate existing ideas and values, and marketing-led approaches, which typically advocate small actions and green consumerism without accounting for larger-scale and longer-term consequences. However, environmentalists articulate the need for rapid and radical change, which is already taking place in many parts of the world. Further, we have been inspired by instances of what might be called 'radical incrementalism', or change movements arising from diverse and local responses to extreme or adverse conditions.

Today, the fiscal and technical futures of energy are hot topics in fields such as economics and engineering. Indeed, we need only look to recent tipping points in fuel cost to see an explosion of emerging behavioral and cultural effects. This exposes the extent to which people might be prompted to change, to reevaluate the arrangement of homes and cities, to adjust daily habits and consumer lifestyles, and to develop new social formations for coping with transitions to new ways of life.

We started Energy Futures by adapting some methods from futures studies in order to open up new ways of identifying and imagining the potentials for such change. Based on methods such as 'environmental scanning', we started by spotting trends in perceptions and behaviors around energy. This involved a search of secondary sources to collect information about such trends and an organizational practice of identifying, analyzing and mapping trends in relation to one another.

For example, we collected examples of consumer and (sub)cultural reactions to rising fuel costs and examined forecasts of energy futures and tipping points by economists and scientists. Based on our collected documentation of today's trends and future scenarios, we also began to identify and discuss issues that seemed to influence perceptions and behaviors. Changes in contextual factors surfaced, such as cost and economy, governmental rhetoric and policy, individual and collective values, consumer information and communication, technology and media developments, emerging products and services, etc.

While we had intended to pick one topic to pursue, we discovered that it was the relation among multiple trends and forecasts, and the combination of issues involved, that seemed to point to substantial potentials for wider change. Choosing one, or proposing a new one, seemed only to reduce or deny competing or complementary trends and the wider range of issues involved.

Instead, we decided to pursue three directions — which we called Fuel Costs Rise, 2000 Watt Diet and Rolling Blackouts. Each was extrapolated as a scenario from real-life examples, framed in order to develop different sets of the issues identified. Each was elaborated in terms of contextual factors, including societal, political and material/technical implications. In terms of futures studies, this might be seen in relation to methods for exploring trends in 'exploratory forecasting'.

These scenarios allowed us to frame complex issues without over-simplification, as well as to point to potential implications that were both speculative and specific. While we were already starting to imagine possible design directions, we wanted to further anchor the scenarios in socio-cultural terms before shifting to the technical and material terms of design. To do this, we developed a method we called 'real fiction' for playing out what the scenarios could mean for different people. This was based on a combination of techniques from user-centered design

Energy Futures

VOLUNTARY SIMPLICITY

CLIMATE
REFUGEES

GREEN SUMMER
SITES

BUY BACK
SCHEMES

OUTLAW WAST

SLOW TRAVEL

HELIOTROPISM

NEON PIRATES

HYPERMILING

GOOD ENERGY

SEASONLESS
FASHION

ECO-ISLAM

VERTICAL
FARMING

ECO-DISOBEDIENCE

SHARED OWNERSHIP

SCHEDULED BLACKOUTS
END GAME SCENARIOS
EATING LOCAL
PARIS PLAGE
(S)LOW TOURISM
SHARE-A-RIDE
LIVABILITY INDEX
WALK SCORE
SELF-SERVICE TRAM
TIDY PROFIT
POST-CARBON CITIES
PLASTIC-BAG BAN
DARK-SKY
EARTH HOUR
HEAT WAVE
LOANING
FRACTIONAL LIVING

(personas), market research (values modes) and personal interviews with friends and family.

Adam, Antoine and Anna were three different characters developed to be both real and familiar as well as diverse and generalizable. To bring these characters to life, we created a game-like structure based on role-plays of each scenario. We also introduced situations related to common issues in sustainable development, which we named 'foot-in-the-door', 'rebound effect' and 'what you say (versus) do'. Combining characters as roles and situations as plot points, we played out the scenarios exploring both short-term reactions and long-term adaptations. This allowed us to imagine diverse energy futures in a rich and elaborate way — wider contextual issues could be raised and debated from the plural viewpoints of the characters.

This series of methods allowed us to gain a rapid understanding of a wide range of developments and issues, as well as to begin to locate more concrete potentials for interventions. While the scanning activity seemed to open up for complexity and contradiction, we could start to empathize in a more personal way with different views through the 'real fiction' method even as the game-play started to locate evocative sites, situations and artifacts.

• **Fuel Costs Rise**
...above a critical threshold. Everything becomes more costly, and travel is prohibitively expensive. Issues: new work week, class and gendered commuting patterns, short-haul travel, holiday planning.

• **2000 Watt Diet**
Average per capita energy consumption is 2000W globally — but 6000W in Europe. Governments support a 'diet' scheme — citizens gain rights through cooperation. Issues: local power and collective bargaining, location-based contracts and personal allowances.

• **Rolling Blackouts**
Demand for electricity outstrips supply — electricity is rationed by district and time zone. Issues: freeloading and corruption, lifestyle corridors and incentive zoning, dark tourism and slow-lane living.

Adam - *Pioneer*

"I have always sniffed my way through the urban jungle."

"I have always sniffed my way through the urban jungle," says Adam, a southern Californian of Jewish-Italian heritage (he found out he was adopted as a teenager). Adam has a BA in history and toured around Europe extensively. He decided to settle down in Vienna, where he met his Turkish girlfriend. Adam has always been interested in politics and art, so he was involved with the Viennese art world, at first through his girlfriend, who was studying there. The couple decided to move to Istanbul after Eda finished her studies. It was Adam who insisted. Adam says he has always been attracted to non-Western cultures and moving from well-structured Central Europe to Istanbul was the best thing he did with his life. He says that art and media industries were flourishing when he first came to Istanbul in the mid-1990's, still undiscovered by the 'Westerners'. "There is a huge influx of Westerners and the expat community here is really established now. I am lucky to be the early bird," he adds.

Adam clearly enjoys his network in the cosmopolitan setting, although he feels the urge to make frequent countryside visits. His last trip was in South East Turkey and Syria, backpacking. He had been photographing the region extensively and he is deeply interested in the Sufi order of Islamic mysticism. He got himself invited to rituals, and he is happy that they accepted him as a family member in an ancient clan.

Adam is also a practicing media artist and does VJ-ing with his partner as a side job. He is mostly involved in the ethnic/electronic music scene. His art and media collective developed a digital imaging tool through which he produces his media work. He regularly blogs about subjects ranging from politics, activism, media and art.

Antoine - Prospector

"As everyone does, I feel concerned about the Amazon and wildlife... However I'm not very attentive to recycling, I make the effort because of my roommate."

Demographic Profile
Age: 21
Family Size: 3
Shares housing with 2 other students in Paris Est (cheap side)
Education: BA graduate
Nationality: French
Social Class: Middle class. His parents used to own
a restaurant but are now retired and live in Provence.

Antoine comes from a small town in the South of France, where he grew up with his elder brother. When he was little, he wished he could be a superhero – admired and invincible. He learned how to play the drums and joined his brother and friends in a band, playing gigs in the local area.

At 18, he decided to study political science and was accepted at the prestigious Dauphine university in Paris. After graduating, he decided to continue studying and is now pursuing a Masters in economics and marketing. He doesn't know what career he will pursue but imagines himself as a politician or a music producer.

Debates on global issues and climate change are often organised during classes. "As everyone does, I feel concerned about the Amazon and wildlife... However I'm not very attentive to recycling, I make the effort because of my room-mate." He went along when his friends joined the guerilla group 'Neon Pirates', terrorists who roam around at night switching off neon lights and the lights in shop windows to save energy. "We are well-known in the neighbourhood now!". In 2007, 'Velib' was launched in Paris – Antoine followed the trend by getting his own bicycle. He cycles to university everyday and then to André Citroen public park – "a good place to be seen in!". Antoine has a new project in mind: a student exchange to California next year.

Anna - *Settler*

"I'm going to take mum to Chelsea flower show!! Actually quite excited... Is that sad? Definitely not rock and roll!"

Demographic Profile

Age: 27
Family Size: 2 (and a dog)
Lives in a semi-detached house in Somerset, UK
Education: University graduate
Nationality: British
Social Class: Middle class, conservative leanings

Anna was born and grew up in Street, Somerset, a small town founded by the shoemaker Clarks for their workers. Her father, Steve, ran a successful IT business while her mother, Catherine, looked after Anna and her brother James. Anna attended local schools, where she made some life-long friends, and met her future husband, Vickery.

Anna studied arts-based subjects, doing well in English and Art. She continued her relationship with Vickery, though they went to different universities – Anna went to Portsmouth university to study fashion and Vickery to Bristol to read law.

After graduation, she was offered a job in London but turned it down, deciding instead to move back to her home town of Street. She married Vickery when she was 24, and together they bought a house in Street – the same village where her parents, a grandparent and her husband's parents still live. They have a dog and take it for a walk in the field five minutes down the road everyday. There is a little community of dog-walkers there, and they cook dog biscuits for presents at Christmas.

Anna drives to work in Minehead everyday, where she is a designer at a leather-ware company. Her friends mostly live locally, and when they go on holiday, it's mostly camping by a beach in England.

She wears a small Christian cross around her neck, but she isn't practising. She is now 27 years old.

She prefers being comfortable over adventure. She is practically-minded, and isn't particularly interested in 'alternative' culture. She trusts authority and assumes it works in her interest. She shares general concerns about 'the environment' when they arise but doesn't give it much thought, as it rarely impinges on her day-to-day life. She plans to have her first child in two years, when her and her husband will be more financially secure.

2000 Watt Diet
Adam, 38 (Pioneer)

Pioneers are society's scouts, testing and innovating, questioning.
They may be strongly ethical or more relaxed, into 'doing their own thing'.

Which means Adam values self-esteem, personal growth, mobility, flexibility. He is typically modest, solitary, inquisitive, unplanned, non-acquisitive, and original.

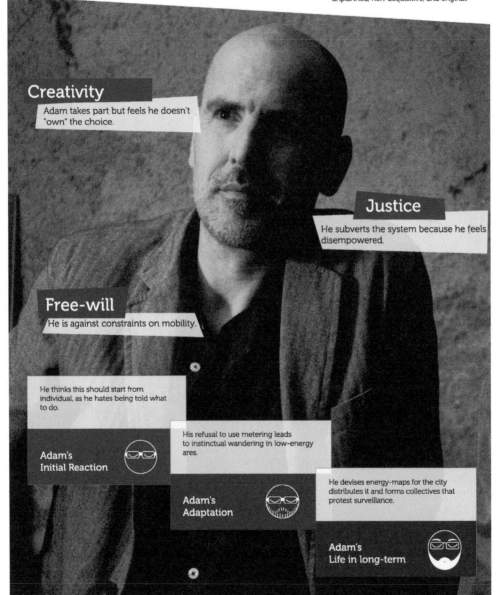

Creativity
Adam takes part but feels he doesn't "own" the choice.

Justice
He subverts the system because he feels disempowered.

Free-will
He is against constraints on mobility.

He thinks this should start from individual, as he hates being told what to do.

Adam's Initial Reaction

His refusal to use metering leads to instinctual wandering in low-energy ares.

Adam's Adaptation

He devises energy-maps for the city distributes it and forms collectives that protest surveillance.

Adam's Life in long-term

Rolling Blackouts
Antoine, 21 (Prospector)

Prospectors are outer-directed. They want to be seen succeed and want to display the symbols of success in eveything they do.

Antoine seeks social recognition and likes to be with the 'in crowd' but is independant enough to not just follow blindly.

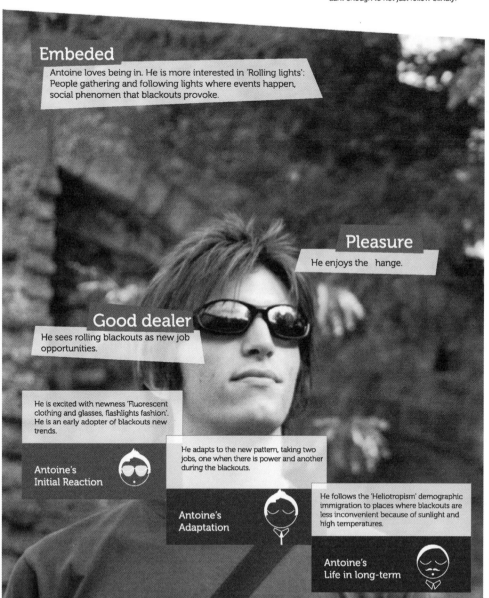

Embeded

Antoine loves being in. He is more interested in 'Rolling lights': People gathering and following lights where events happen, social phenomen that blackouts provoke.

Pleasure

He enjoys the hange.

Good dealer

He sees rolling blackouts as new job opportunities.

He is excited with newness 'Fluorescent clothing and glasses, flashlights fashion'. He is an early adopter of blackouts new trends.

Antoine's Initial Reaction

He adapts to the new pattern, taking two jobs, one when there is power and another during the blackouts.

Antoine's Adaptation

He follows the 'Heliotropism' demographic immigration to places where blackouts are less inconvenient because of sunlight and high temperatures.

Antoine's Life in long-term

Fuel Costs Rise
Anna, 27 (Settler)

Settlers are socially conservative, seeking stability and valuing routine, the known, the local. They tend to trust authority and stick to the rules.

Anna's main concerns are her family, her home, and being comfortable.

Stability

She is concerned about job security. The rise in fuel costs means she must work from home, going to the workplace just two days a month. Her husband now sometimes stays at his office for a few nights in a row.

Guilt

Her husband has to work a bit harder, but she secretly quite likes aspects of the new situation. Communitites become closer and more insular confriming her basic norms.

Complacency

Though effected by the rise in prices her household is ok. The increase in home entertainment and new services focussing on the local suits her lifestyle.

Concerned for her and her husband's job security.

Anna's Initial Reaction

Commuter patterns change. Her husband commutes less but stays over at work for days at a time.

Anna's Adaptation

She takes advantage of people's slower travel by turning part of her home in to a guest house.

Anna's Life in long-term

Proposing designs for transition

Design has long played a role in future speculation. For example, the 'concept car', 'future city' and 'ideal home' are genres displayed in trade shows and world expositions, typically envisioning a future that affirms the premises of certain ways of life, social ideals and new technologies. In science fiction and popular media visions of environmental and planetary futures, design might illustrate a darker and even a disastrous view. Whether utopic or dystopic, design gives form to persuasive 'visions of the future'. Typically bound into larger projects with a more or less overt function to advertise or entertain, such visions operate to persuade or dissuade an audience about a specific set of ideas or ideals.

In such terms, concept design and visionary architecture have the potential to operate in ways not unlike the forecasts and scenarios produced within the field of futures studies. In addition to common applications (such as retirement planning, city development or corporate strategy), futures studies can also take issue with the way things are, mapping out the potentially radical implications of climate change, global conflicts, consumption trends and grassroots movements. Instead of accurate predictions or complete descriptions, forecasts and scenarios often articulate multiple, competing and extreme futures — in order to situate a discussion, in the present, about what is possible, preferable or desirable.

In Energy Futures, we were interested in how design might operate more along the lines of methods in futures studies. In this way, we wanted to move away from the tendency of designed visions of the future to be 'one-liners' — simplistic statements intended to shock or sell, or select narratives suppressing real-life complexity and diversity. We were also critcial of how such visions tend to operate in sustainable design — both eco-topia and eco-horror genres paint a picture of the future, but without any discussion of what it would be like live in it or what it would take to get there. We took possible energy futures, including extremes and far-futures as a point of departure. But, as we moved on to design, we focused on what might happen in the transition between now and then.

How might responses look in different places and among diverse groups? What kinds of adaptations and disruptions might appear? How might artifacts, technologies, services, policies, procedures, habits and traditions take shape along the way? These questions framed our design brief — situating and articulating transitions to possible futures.

In relation to our three scenarios, we developed many design concepts located along potential paths for transitioning to such futures. Combining forecasting with backcasting methods, we created a rough map and timeline for locating the concepts in relation to one another, and to different situations and temporal scales.

From among these design concepts, we selected five to elaborate further. These were developed both as artifacts and as stories, in which the artifacts were embedded. For us, this was essential to escape the one-liner, to bring static images and still-life models alive. While, on one hand, the stories were told in terms of a specific place or person, they also were intended to stand for larger projections of possible evolutions in belief and behavior and possible transformations in local material and technical systems. Each concept was developed as a set of physical and communication materials, intended to evoke a sort of real-life fiction about Energy Futures.

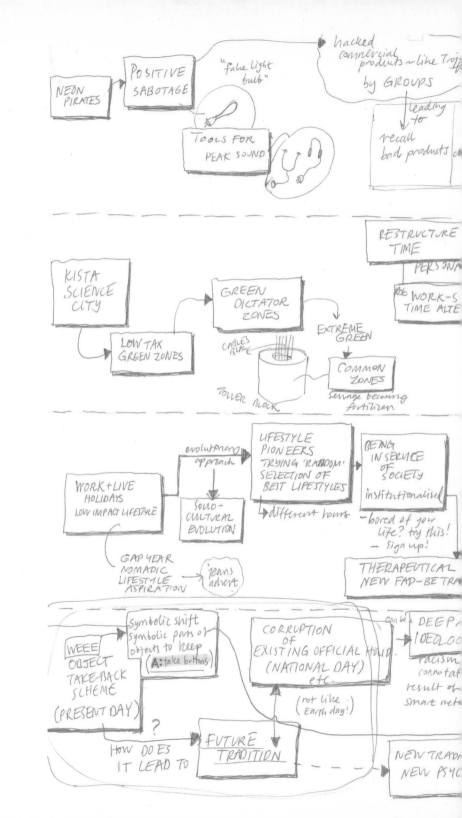

NEON PIRATES

POSITIVE SABOTAGE

"fake light bulb"

TOOLS FOR PEAK SOUND

hacked commercial products ~ like Troj[...] by GROUPS

leading to recall bad products [...]

RESTRUCTURE TIME
PERSONA[...]

[...] WORK-S[...]
TIME ALTE[...]

KISTA SCIENCE CITY

LOW TAX GREEN ZONES

GREEN DICTATOR ZONES

EXTREME GREEN

CABLES [...]

COMMON ZONES

TOWER BLOCK

sewage becoming fertilizer

WORK+LIVE HOLIDAYS
LOW IMPACT LIFESTYLE

evolutionary approach

SOCIO-CULTURAL EVOLUTION

LIFESTYLE PIONEERS TRYING 'RANDOM' SELECTION OF BEST LIFESTYLES

different hours

BEING IN SERVICE OF SOCIETY
institutionalised

- bored of your life? try this!
- Sign up!

GAP YEAR NOMADIC LIFESTYLE ASPIRATION

jeans advert

THERAPEUTICAL NEW FAD-BE TR[...]

WEEE OBJECT TAKE-BACK SCHEME (PRESENT DAY)

symbolic shift symbolic parts of objects to keep
(A: fake buttons)

CORRUPTION OF EXISTING OFFICIAL HOLID. (NATIONAL DAY) etc.

(not like Earth day!)

can be a DEEP[...] IDEOLOG[...]

racism connotat[...] result of smart net[...]

?

HOW DOES IT LEAD TO

FUTURE TRADITION

NEW TRAD[...] NEW PSYC[...]

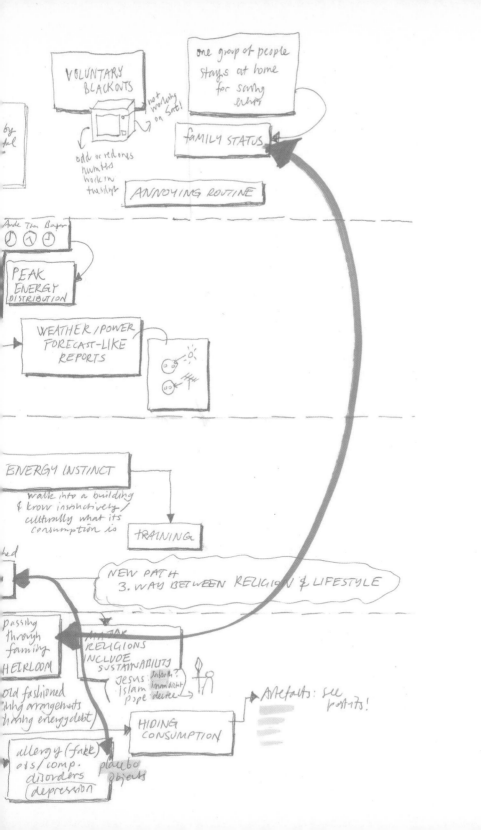

VOLUNTARY BLACKOUTS

not working on Snt!

odd or red ones
numbered
work in twilight

one group of people stays at home for saving energy

by tal

FAMILY STATUS

ANNOYING ROUTINE

Ande Than Bayer

PEAK ENERGY DISTRIBUTION

WEATHER/POWER FORECAST-LIKE REPORTS

ENERGY INSTINCT

walk into a building
& know instinctively/
culturally what its
consumption is

TRAINING

NEW PATH
3. WAY BETWEEN RELIGION & LIFESTYLE

passing
through
family
HEIRLOOM

old fashioned
living arrangements
having energy debt)

MAJOR RELIGIONS INCLUDE SUSTAINABILITY

Jesus
Islam
pope

Sabbath?
immediate
decree

allergy (fake)
ots/comp.
disorders
(depression

placebo
objects

HIDING CONSUMPTION

Artefacts: see
posts!

Socket Bombs

"Socket Bombing is direct action performed as a protest against excessive electricity consumption. It involves purposefully causing a short circuit in a building's electrical mains or light sockets. Consisting only of cheap and rewired electrical hardware and timers, socket bombs are typically planted to target supermarkets, chain stores and corporations. Incidents have been reported in London, Paris, Istanbul and Stockholm. One group managed to cut the power to the majority of shops in Kista Galleria in Sweden on the 6th of September 2008."

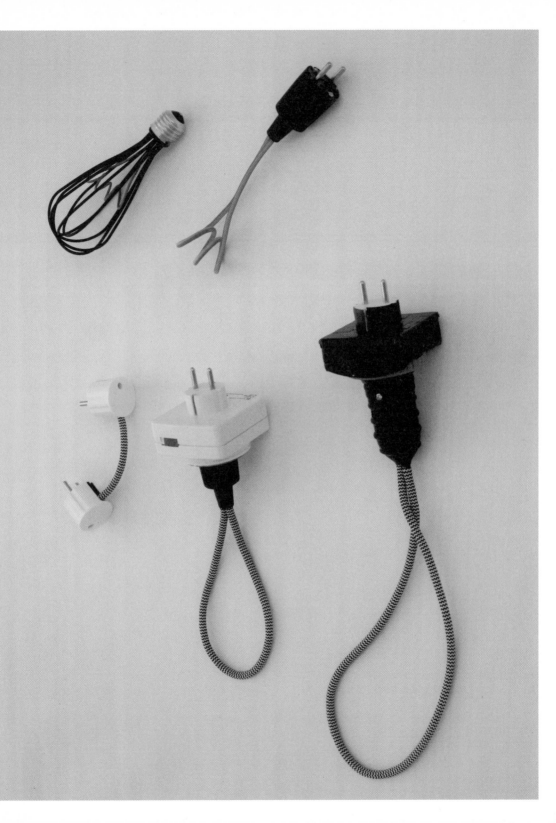

Good morning and welcome.

Here is the Energy Forecast

for today Friday 5th September,

Today the north and middle regions

will have abundant power

from steady winds

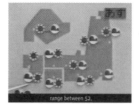
range between 52,

and 134 watts per square metre

Looking into the weekend

things get less energetic.

We wish you an energetic Friday

and a slow and relaxing weekend!

Energy Forecast Report

"And now for the Power Forecast. This afternoon, we'll see some bright sun of about 80W per square meter for around 3 hours, so it'll be a great time to get those appliances working. Things get a bit dimmer towards the weekend with only about 46W per square meter penetrating the clouds, so plan for a quieter Sunday. If you've got the big family lunch planned, you'll have to use dirty power, I'm afraid, as there also won't be much wind."

Voluntary Blackouts

"Before, we were living in a kind of fast-forward dream world — our senses constantly assaulted by all the usual so-called 'modern conveniences' — everything wanted our attention. We didn't know it, but we just didn't have time to think. Then, the power went out for a week, and we found we preferred it. So we decided to move to a Blackout Zone that has electricity for only one hour in the evening. Now, we get more sleep, we spend more time together, we're calmer — it saved our family life!"

B

Blackout Zone

Sunday-Monday

ARE YOU OVERWEIGHT?

At last! Energy Independance *and* Great Looks from just one mildly invasive procedure!

These days we do more, but what we do has changed - instead of grinding corn we crunch numbers! And while no-one told our bodies, there's a supermarket round every corner... so there's just no need to store the excess energy from our food and drink as unsightly fat.

The 'Umbilicus' device updates our bodies for our 21st century environment.

It contains friendly bacteria, engineered to metabolise fats and lipids into electrical energy - power for the devices we rely on for our work and play. So you can eat, drink and be merry, safe in the knowledge your body is putting those calories to work.

Umbilicus - *total energy freedom.*

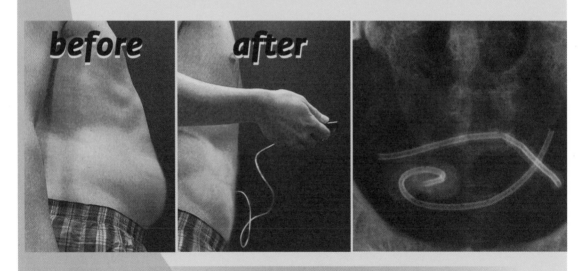

before   after

Umbilical Cord

"At last! Energy Independence and Great Looks from just one mildly invasive procedure! Today, there's no need to store the excess energy from food as unsightly fat. The 'Umbilicus' updates our bodies for our 21st century environment. It contains friendly bacteria, engineered to metabolize fats and lipids into electrical energy — power for the devices we rely on for our work and play. Eat, drink and be merry — knowing that your body is putting those calories to work!"

Future Tradition

"Today, we celebrate our penance. Today we mustn't use power. We know we're not perfect, but we keep on trying. So we wrap our needy objects to resist temptation! And we gather outside and together turn the sky red!"

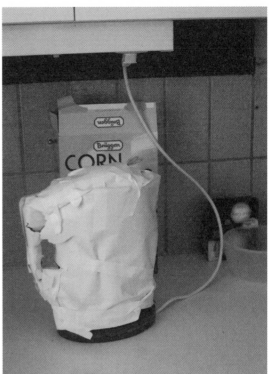

Performing energy futures

The design concepts were not intended as ends in themselves, but for staging discussions with stakeholders about potential energy futures in the here and now. For such purposes, we developed methods to frame and stage such a discussion, inspired by workshop and game methods from participatory design and futures studies as well as by relational and performative techniques in art.

Since we were interested in opening up, rather than resolving or closing options, we felt it was important to let the diverse design concepts co-exist. However, in order that the concepts might speak for themselves, we created a meta-narrative, or (super)fiction, about living within the potential futures. We developed this as a script for a performance, in which stakeholders themselves discover the concepts and discuss the futures. So far, we have staged one 'opening' performance in a gallery. Reversing expectations about openings and exhibits typical in such a setting, this exhibition unfolds over time and depends upon the visitors' actions. Those of us behind the creation and curation of the project were mostly absent.

These were tactics intended to invite — and require — participation in interpreting and making sense of these strangely familiar Energy Futures. We wanted to stage a situation in which people might examine their assumptions, discuss alternatives and declare their objectives.

The doors open at 18:00. The gallery is empty and bare
— but drinks are served, visitors begin to gather and meet.
By invitation only, the visitors include designers, architects,
educators, engineers and historians. After some time,
they begin to look around for the organizers, to wonder
whether this is, in fact, an opening at all. A mobile phone
rings — someone excuses themselves from a conversation
to answer. Suddenly, everyone is reaching for their ringing
or vibrating phone — they answer, and all of them hear the
same greeting.

Hello!
Can everyone hear me OK? There'll be time for questions at the
end, but if you can't hear me then please say so... Right! I know
you were expecting an exhibition but, well, we've really just
got research. That's what's in the case you can see there on the
table... If you all go over there and open the case, you'll see some
envelopes and objects — I'll tell you a little more about these.

Energy Futures are closely linked to the looming future
of climate change.

Usually, we see either eco-horror from a post-crash world
or 3D renderings of bright new technologies for some sort of future
eco-topia. We've tried to stay away from these extremes in our
research. But, where technology is concerned, the future comes
around quickly. In avoiding the extremes, perhaps we've not
gone far enough? In fact, we found that most of the things we
researched about energy futures already exist in one form
or another. So, all we can do is present our findings...

If you open envelopes 1 to 4... and get out and open the
laptop with the number 5... These are 'socket bombs', made
according to instructions we found on a website. The loops of
wire cause a short-circuit, which causes the circuit breakers to
trip, cutting the power to sockets in a building. The bombers
use timers so they can get away — you can read about how
they work on the laptop — just open a web browser and look

it up on Wikipedia. So, it seems that energy consumption is becoming politicized. Do they target institutions who use energy 'wastefully', or those that buy their electricity from sources to which they object? Is it strange that access to electricity is so unguarded?

We downloaded the next thing from YouTube — we had to get a friend to translate it into English, you can see the movie on the laptop labelled 7... In envelope 8, there's something we found at the Clas Ohlson hardware store...

We printed these photos out from Flickr — someone's wrapped all their electrical appliances at home. We tried it out and it's quite fun — see the wrapped object 10 and 11, 12 and 13... The wrapping is part of some sort of tradition, a kind of Earth Day — a reminder to not buy more unnecessary things, the things stay wrapped for the three months before Christmas, which is celebrated by unwrapping the things you already have. There's apparently a story they tell the kids, about a Sun that gets jealous of all the electric lights and gizmos, and so they have to wrap them all up to stop the sun getting angry and hot. CAREFUL — Don't pull the string as you get out object 12. It's something for turning the sky red — I think that's meant to be something about making the atmosphere visible. Read the label on the object out loud...

If you open 14, you'll see an example of a kind of sign that my aunt was telling me about. Planned blackouts are common in parts of the developing world to share the limited power available — why not live with such limits elsewhere? My aunt lives in Wellington (I'm half New Zealandish, did you know?), in some kind of new zone — there's some snapshots she sent me in the envelope...

In envelope 15, there's something you can take home with you to ask your healthcare professional about. Will new and advanced technologies save us from our own bad habits?

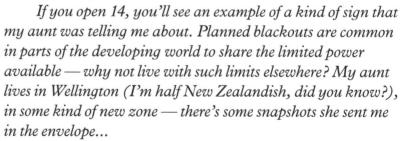

The suitcase contains a series of envelopes and objects, each labeled with a number. An absent guide speaks via a multi-party telephone call. Listening, the visitors unpack the suitcase, opening envelopes and spreading out the artifacts. They watch the YouTube videos and browse entries on Wikipedia. Further descriptions are provided in a booklet that refers to the numbered artifacts. Sometimes, these conflict with the personal account given over the phone; open-ended questions are inserted here and there as provocations. Visitors read different parts of the material out loud to one another and interpret things in different ways, occasionally erupting into a sort of improvised debate. A sort of 'oral history' builds up over time out of fragments, between and across multiple accounts and interpretations — ending up in another, collective discourse.

Over the course of an hour, the contents of the case have taken over the gallery space, an exhibition unpacked and arranged in the course of the phone call. Amongst themselves, the visitors have had to collaborate to unfold and make sense of these Energy Futures. Emerging along the way were a variety of intimate stories and personal opinions, as well as political issues and professional points of view. Eventually, three of the researchers, one of which was on the other end of the telephone call, come into the gallery. They mingle with the visitors, joining into local discussions around the artifacts and discussing how these energy futures might come to be — and what it might mean if they did.

43

Energy FuturesEnergy Futures

Energy Futures is part of Switch!, a design research program at the Interactive Institute sponsored by the Swedish Energy Agency.

Project team Ramia Mazé, Aude Messager, Thomas Thwaites, Basar Önal

Additional credit for photo on p.37 Johannes Tolk

Further reading Ramia Mazé and Basar Önal, "Hands on the Future," in *Proceedings of the Stockholm Futures Conference* (Stockholm: unpublished, 2010).

3Ecologies

Martin Avila, John Carpenter,
Ramia Mazé

'3Ecologies' makes visible factors affecting the sustainability of consumer products. Including environmental, sociological and psychological factors in production and consumption, 3Ecologies challenges prevalent models of sustainability to emphasize human agency and consequences. Sustainability is mapped over time — as histories and potential futures of products — through lifespan and extended lifecycle(s). Under development as an open-source internet application, graphical eco-labeling scheme and interactive museum installation, 3Ecologies develops novel techniques for dynamic information visualization, interactive story-telling and user interaction. By providing a long view upon the 'life' of things we might ordinarily take for granted, the project aims to engage a broad audience in ecological thinking.

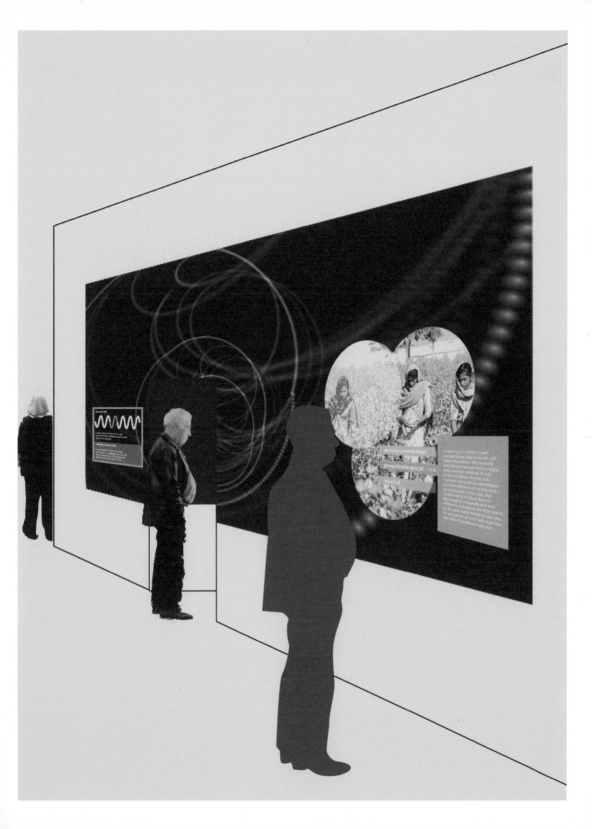

Modelling product sustainability

3Ecologies visualizes factors that impact the sustainability of durable and non-durable consumer goods. The production and consumption of goods such as clothing, furniture, toys, appliances, cars, food and packaging involves energy, chemicals, waste and emissions. In addition to the fact that industry is under increasing political directives and economic imperatives to consider such environmental factors, there is a substantial and increasing consumer demand for knowledge, choice and change. We must further understand and communicate about sustainability both in terms of the products that we make — and the decisions that we take as consumers.

There are several existing ways to model sustainability factors. For example, the 'triple bottom line' accounts for environmental factors as part of financial metrics; 'lifecycle assessment' calculates variables in terms of raw materials, resources and emissions associated with consumer products, and; 'blueprinting' attempts to incorporate the value chains and information flows of businesses and institutions. Stemming from economic and environmental science, these models either tend to take schematic forms, such as process chains and matrix audits, or very complex statistical charts and quantitative graphs. Resulting abstraction and complexity, however, entails that their use is typically limited to engineers and managers, with only limited accessibility to design, marketing, consumers and the public.

3Ecologies is a response to rapidly growing interest in and demand for information about the environmental costs and consequences of consumer goods — and to the gap in the set of available tools (including both modeling techniques and visualization technologies) for communicating sustainability factors and actionable choices available to designers and consumers.

The project started with the development of two basic conceptual models, which can be applied to analyze, communicate and forecast discrete factors impacting upon the sustainability of a given artifact.

The first is based on the cyclical model common in 'lifecycle assessment' and 'cradle-to-grave' thinking. This model plots key points along the path typically followed by a consumer product, from material sources in nature and agriculture, to parts and product manufacture, to retail and consumer choices at the point-of-purchase, to events throughout the use and lifespan of a product, to the multiple options at the point of disposal.

The second is a conceptual model that articulates inter-relations among three sets of factors determining the sustainability of consumer products — psychological, sociological and environmental. This is based on principles set out in Felix Guattari's book *The Three Ecologies*[1].

We have developed this latter model to extend and challenge the 'triple bottom line' — a model that identifies economic, social and environmental factors. In our view, the separation of economy as a separate category obscures the social construction and situated nature of economic factors. Economy is crucial as a standard measure of ecological conditions and of exchange within society — but is bound into particular forms of social interaction and material situations. While considering economy as an underlying principle in all categories of analysis, we foreground, following Guattari, the social and human factors associated with sociology and psychology. This renegotiation of variables within the model enables us to better articulate the influence of individual actors and groups and the impact of perceptions, emotions, values and choices on sustainability.

1 — Felix Guattari, *The Three Ecologies* (London: Athlone Press, 2001).

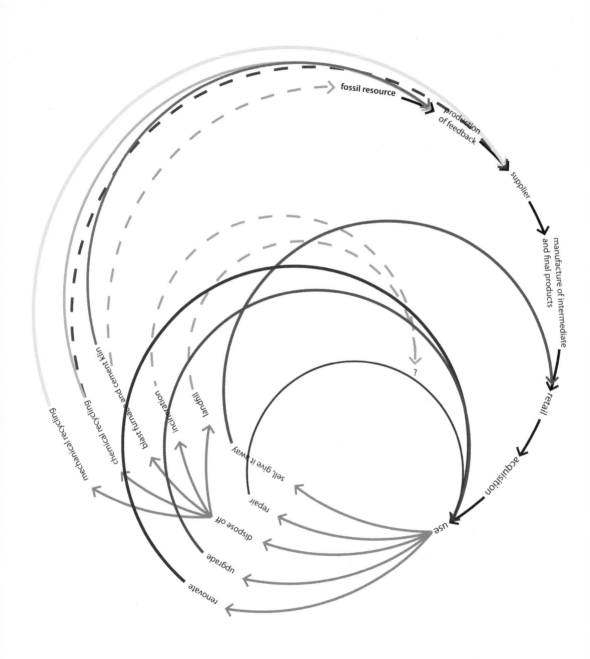

fossil resource

production of feedback

supplier

manufacture of intermediate and final products

retail

acquisition

use

?

mechanical recycling

chemical recycling

blast furnace and cement kiln

incineration

landfill

sell, give it away

repair

dispose off

upgrade

renovate

Switch!

psychological

sociological

environmental

Incorporating three sustainability factors

Rather than conceiving of sustainability as a static or final matter of fact, we consider it as a consequence of multiple factors that interact and change over time.

Consider an ordinary water bottle made of glass or plastic — of course we can say something about sustainability if we examine its basic material components, for instance if they are recyclable or biodegradable. Tracing back to original sources of the materials and conditions of manufacture, we can say something more about environmental factors such as the use of renewable resources, chemical additives or byproducts, energy consumption, transportation, etc. In fact, it is just such aspects that lifecycle assessment typically tries to identify and quantify in terms of standard metrics.

However, there are other crucial factors — including those that may be difficult to isolate and measure, that vary over time, and that depend upon other actors and circumstances...

What about the working conditions in farms and factories, impacts on personal economy, societal welfare and cultural heritage? At point-of-purchase, what about consumer perceptions, gendered buying habits, peer pressure or brand experience? During use, what about attachment, status and trends? What about the factors impinging upon disposal, such as loss and breakage, consumer information or local services? How do we consider gifts, inheritance, donations and reclamation? Does it change things if we know that a bottle has been refilled hundreds of times, that a fleece jacket is derived from discarded plastic bottles, that the insulating and aesthetic properties of glass bottles make them an ideal building material for homes and shelters in the developing world?

In 3Ecologies, we have particularly focused on how such human factors might be considered and expressed.

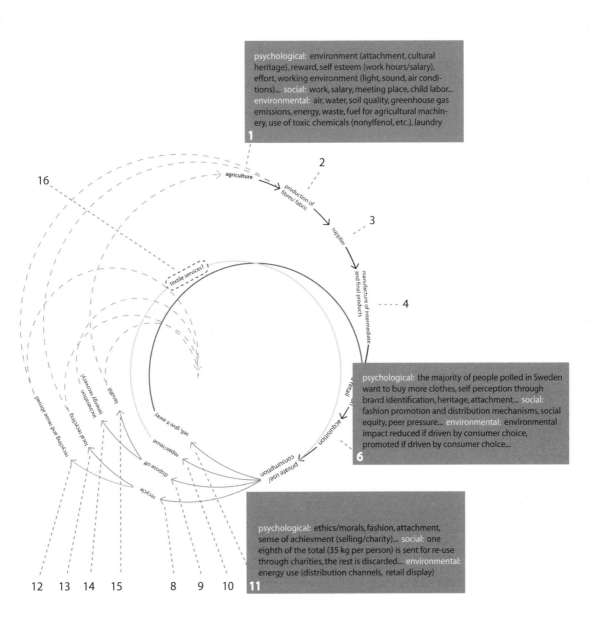

psychological: environment (attachment, cultural heritage), reward, self esteem (work hours/salary), effort, working environment (light, sound, air conditions)... social: work, salary, meeting place, child labor... environmental: air, water, soil quality, greenhouse gas emissions, energy, waste, fuel for agricultural machinery, use of toxic chemicals (nonylfenol, etc.), laundry

1

2

16

agriculture

production of fibres/ fabric

supplier

3

textile services?

manufacture of intermediate and final products

4

psychological: the majority of people polled in Sweden want to buy more clothes, self perception through brand identification, heritage, attachment... social: fashion promotion and distribution mechanisms, social equity, peer pressure... environmental: environmental impact reduced if driven by consumer choice, promoted if driven by consumer choice...

6

retail

acquisition

private use/ consumption

repair/reuse

sell/give it away

dispose off

recycle

landfill

incineration (energy recovery)

local recycling

recycling and reuse abroad

psychological: ethics/morals, fashion, attachment, sense of achievment (selling/charity)... social: one eighth of the total (35 kg per person) is sent for re-use through charities, the rest is discarded... environmental: energy use (distribution channels, retail display)

12   13   14   15   8   9   10   **11**

Developing sustainable production and consumption practices is complex, since it requires consideration of multiple and interacting factors over long periods of time. If these can be expressed, people might better understand how their actions can have an effect. In our model, individuals and social groups are considered alongside the other factors affecting an artifact during its lifecycle(s). From this basis, mapping out a wide range of possible actions and interactions might help to generate a better picture of potential values, influences and circumstances involved. For example, we might imagine and anticipate possible future effects of decisions made by designers. Further, if we can communicate key decision points during pre- and post-consumption, we might increase self-reflection and empowerment among consumers.

As an information visualization, 3Ecologies has been developed as a dynamic and interactive tool for people to trace the consequences of different decisions. The basic models behind the design of the visualization are the lifecycle diagram and the depiction of psychological, sociological and environmental factors traced through one or more lifecycles. The visualization is based on data behind each of the models and relations among the factors at key points along the lifecycle(s). One important implication of this is that the lifecycle diagram shifts from being a circular or cyclical form to one that continually evolves. Neither environmental nor psychological and sociological conditions can be returned to the same state as at the point of origin, any further lifecycle(s) starts from and generates new conditions. In this way, we move from expressing sustainability in terms of static schematics or a final form to a system that transforms — and is transformed by human factors — over time.

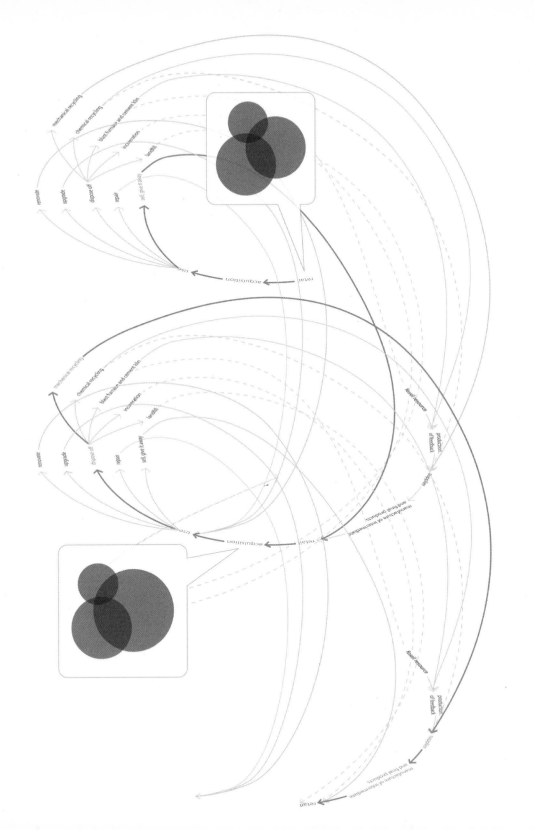

mechanical recycling

chemical recycling

blast furnace and cement kiln

incineration

landfill

sell, give it away

repair

renovate

upgrade

dispose off

use

acquisition

retail

mechanical recycling

chemical recycling

blast furnace and cement kiln

incineration

landfill

sell, give it away

repair

renovate

upgrade

dispose off

use

acquisition

retail

manufacture of intermediate
and final products

production
of feedback

fossil resource

production
of feedback

fossil resource

manufacture of intermediate
and final products

retail

Sketching spatial and temporal aspects

Further breaking from the static nature of typical representations of sustainability, we have also developed narrative techniques. Indeed, methods for storytelling involving visual, verbal and textual elements have proved to be a powerful educational and persuasive technique in the discourse within sustainable development.

To generate ideas for how this might look and feel, our design development process unfolded as a series of graphical and interactive sketches. These mapped the two models in relation to one another and illustrated key points along the lifecycle trajectory over time. At this point, we began sketching extensively within the software programming environment Processing, which operates according to open source principles and is custom built by and for art and design communities.

From our initial concepts, the process evolved through collaborative sketching. Each of the project team comes from a different creative discipline, which entailed that this hands-on activity was a means of communicating ideas to one another and generating new ideas together. Since we were often working at a distance, even in different countries, sketching happened between meetings by video conference and took place 'live' during the meetings themselves. For example, a prepared mock-up could be circulated during a meeting, then others would capture views and sketch directly on top in order to highlight certain aspects or to discuss next steps in design development. In this way, we have treated sketching as an essential extension of the collaboration that has unfolded both through discussing, meeting and writing.

Our software prototype of the 3Ecologies system traces the past and potential future life of a consumer product, displaying the dynamic balance between the three factors at key points along the way. Multiple views, animated paths and zooming mechanisms convey micro

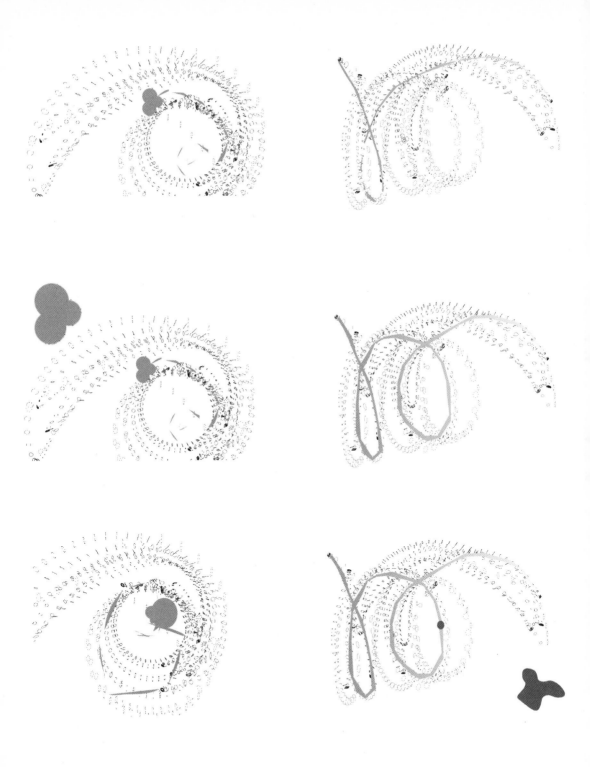

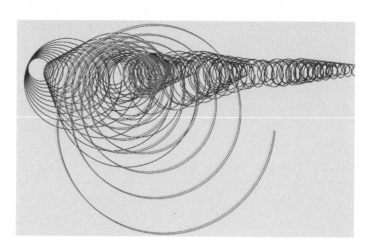

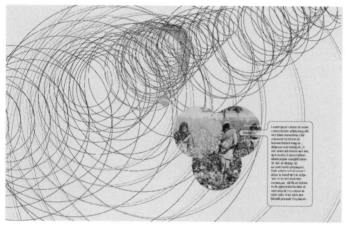

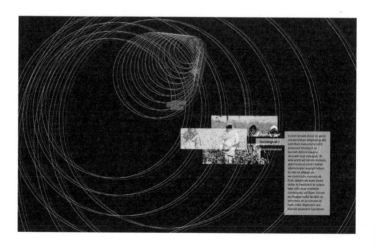

and macro scales, from detailed instances to comprehesive views. To further bring the model to life, multi-media elements at key points convey potential situations and scenarios around the product — tracing through these builds an evocative story over time.

In many narrative tools for communicating sustainability, there is often limited access to the data behind, and linear and non-interactive presentations entail that it can be difficult to display the more complex range of values and choices that are inevitably involved in processes of production and consumption.

In addition to developing the aesthetics and behaviors of the visualization system, we began to dig into the metrics behind the two basic models and to collect documentary evidence of cases to feature within the story. At this point in the process, we began to shift from exploratory sketching with Processing to more precise modeling, in which we programmed the system to calculate and generate parametric relations between the variable components over time. In parallel, we developed more precise diagrams to organize the data in relation to graphical and narrative elements. While earlier sketches concentrated on the aesthetics of the system, these attended to the logics of the structures behind, which were later resolved in a new way.

While most sustainability models tend to focus on the past life of a product, our approach also takes ongoing consumption and future use into consideration. We have explicitly included scenarios of accidental futures and potential (mis/re-)uses of products in order to explore the effects of personal actions and (sub)cultural appropriations. Our explicit investigation of unpredictable elements, transformations over time and potential disruptions relates to current thinking in systems thinking and forecasting applied to sustainability in which chance, risk and resilience are critical aspects.

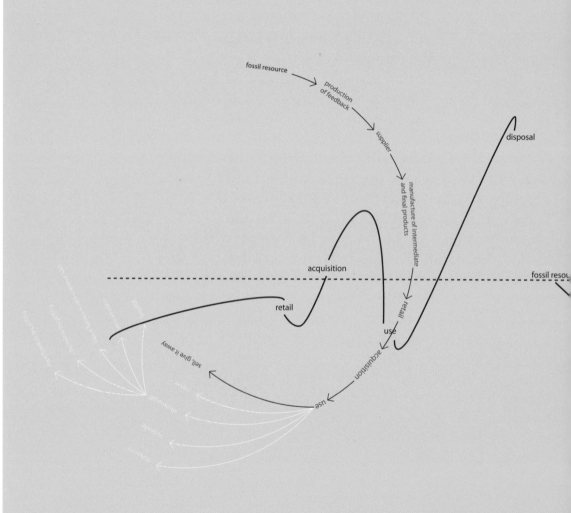

fossil resource

production
of feedback

supplier

manufacture of intermediate
and final products

disposal

acquisition

retail

retail

use

fossil resou

acquisition

use

sell, give it away

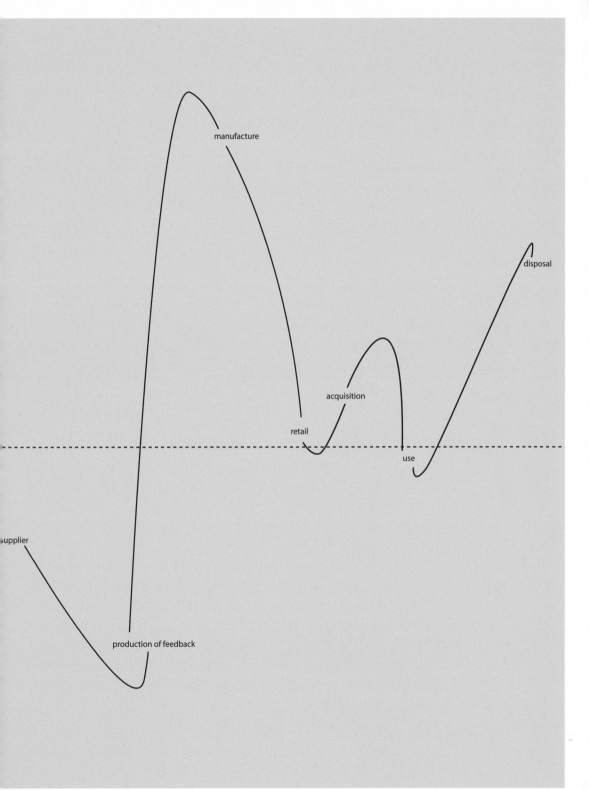

manufacture

disposal

acquisition

retail

use

supplier

production of feedback

At each point along product lifecycle(s), 3Ecologies exposes the histories and potentialities that affect sustainability, presenting these both over time and framed within a more holistic view over three domains of impact and effect. Including 'soft' human factors, decisions and risk, our model, unlike traditional ones, cannot rely on direct data and scientific metrics to the same extent — indeed, there are many questions about validity when it comes to identifying and quantifying such factors.

One way that we have handled this is to think in terms of proportional relationships between the three ecologies, rather than attempting to separate and pin each down to any absolute value — further developing such relations would be an important area for future work. Second is a narrative approach, which represents an alternative priority to that of attempting to capture a complete picture of the entirety of variables. Instead, we analyze events and transitions along the lifecycle(s), plotting a selection of key points. These frame and situate issues in particular instances, such that 'hard' data and 'soft' factors can be better identified and elaborated.

A third, and important, strategy has been to develop the project through case studies of specific products. From the start, problematics of consumer product design and development motivated the project. In addition, we see common products as a way to invite people into the system by focusing on something familiar and everyday. We considered a range of products that are meaningful to our target audiences — for example, in a Swedish context, we considered products of major telecom, automotive and fashion industries as well as ubiquitous products such as water bottles, IKEA icons and well-known architectural objects. Indeed, we have identified several products with both local and global relevance that would be interesting to pursue further.

In order to base our first prototype on substantial data and research already in existence, we have made an initial selection. In particular, we have drawn on research and strategy at Naturskyddsföreningen, or the Swedish Society for Nature Conservation, which is an influential organization that assesses environmental issues, sets eco-label standards and spreads knowledge about sustainability. For this initial design and prototype development, we have targeted the textile sector and, as our first product case and dataset, a cotton T-shirt.

The textile sector is interesting since it has long accounted for both function and fashion (technical and socio-aesthetic) aspects. In relation to trends such as 'fast fashion', in which retailers rotate stock quickly and fashion companies produce ever more variety of increasingly disposable items, Swedish textile and fashion sectors have been increasingly engaged in discussing sustainability and social responsibility. The major categories of clothing products, both by value and mass, are trousers, pullovers and T-shirts.

Our next step was a search through primary and secondary sources for relevant data about the textile and fashion industries as well as typical and potential factors influencing production, consumption and disposal. The T-shirt has proven to be an interesting case since there is a great deal of previous scientific and economic data that we have incorporated, as well as documentary evidence of sociological and psychological linkages to issues in global industrial trade, popular culture, consumer trends and environmental policy.

For example, agriculture and manufacturing of textile goods involves a variety of local social and gender issues, as well as national quotas and labor policies, acquisition and consumption of clothing are heavily influenced by brand and 'fast fashion' trends and, after disposal, there are further lifecycles through reclamation, renewal and reselling on second-hand markets and throughout the developing world.

Based on our collected data and documentary examples, we developed a series of scenarios around key points along the lifecycles of a T-shirt. These were detailed through diagrams plotting relevant data and examples for each key point and through supplemental texts, images and videos illustrating associated issues and human factors. Implemented within the software prototype, a scenario is activated as a user reaches a key point along the lifecycle — making a choice to throw the T-shirt away or give it to charity, for example, diverts the user into scenarios that illustrate the consequences of their decision as well as opening onto possible future potentials and further choices for acting.

2 — Andreas Prevodnik, *T-tröjor med ett smutsigt förflutet* (Stockholm: Naturskyddsföreningen, 2008).

Pepper/Selected Homme
Made in Turkey, 250 kr

Weekday/Cheap Monday
Made in China, 150 kr

Dressman/Batistini
Made in Turkey, 99 kr

Filippa K
Made in Portugal, 600 kr

In 2008, 56% of women and 44% of men in Sweden wanted to buy more clothes than they did the preceeding year. How might it effect which they choose to buy and how they launder, care for and dispose of their clothes if they understood that purchasing a 250g cotton T-shirt implies purchasing 1,700g of fossil fuel, depositing 450g of waste in landfill and emitting 4kg of CO_2 into the atmosphere? Such statistics and examples were raised in a 2008 study by Naturskyddsföreningen.[2]

1 agriculture

Story line:
The main raw material of this T-Shirt – cotton – is produced in the United States, involving genetic modification technologies.

Related research studies:
Genetic Engineering of Cotton Contributes to Humanitarian Good
+
Market and Economy of Organic Cotton

E   S   P
80   30   20

3 supply

Story line:
The supply chain involved in US-grown cotton is subsidized to encourage domestic share of the market.

Related research studies:
Double Subsidies of US Cotton Causing Third World to Protest
+
Effects of Import Quotas on Inter-national Textile Trade

E   S   P
40   35   10

4 manufacture

Story line:
Textile mills have historically had a profound effect on local growth, community life, and civic rights.

Related research studies:
Rise and Fall of a T-Shirt Manufacturer
+
The Travels of a T-Shirt in the Global Economy
+
How Slavery Helped Build a World Economy

E   S   P
50   40   25

6 ret

Story li
The co
produc
diverg

Relate
'Craftm
+
Prices
+
Un-eq
T-Shirt

E
50

3 supply

Story line:
Wholesale supply of post-consumer and secondary commodities is big business – used clothing is one of America's major exports to Africa.

Related research studies:
Travels of a T-Shirt
+
Used clothing and rag exporting plant targeted in illegal immigrant bust
+
RecycleNet: The Online Secondary Commodities Exchange

E   S   P
55   35   15

4 manufacture

Story line:
Imported clothing is locally customized by small entrepreneurs – "any self-respecting man knows his way around a needle and thread".

Related research studies:
Amateurs use old textile machinery to dis-assemble and reuse textile fibers
+
Memories and family legacy of rag-collecting

E   S   P
35   45   35

6 retail

Story line:
Everyone from government ministers to laborers purchase used clothing sold at local markets and by travelling peddlers.

Related research studies:
Tracing the 'value chain' of T-Shirt
+
Second hand clothing culture in Africa

E   S   P
5   40   15

7 co

Story
Weste
by ma
signify
conve

Relate
Tracin
+
Value
and m

E
45

identical
ally due to
of retailers.

e than Brand

ost and Price
009 Sale

7 consumption

Story line:
Consumer encounters with products at point-of-purchase are highly influenced by emotions, social trends and brand experience.

Related research studies:
Buyology - Neuroanalysis of Brand Experience
+
Dangers of 'Fast Fashion' Trend
+
T-Shirts with Optimistic Messages have Sales Boom During Recession

E   S   P
5   35   15

7 consumption

Story line:
Long use of garments have an environ-mental impact and ongoing cost domi-nated by the energy used in washing, drying and ironing.

Related research studies:
Well Dressed? Present and Future Sustainability of Clothing and Textiles
+
Neuro-analysis reveals that brand emotions are similar to religious feelings

E   S   P
65   25   35

11 sell/give away

Story line:
Westerners buy clothes in disposable quantities – and donations to charity shops qualify for a tax write-off.

Related research studies:
Tracing the 'Value Chain' of a T-Shirt from New York to Africa
+
Social pressure/roles around recycling (to eliminate garbage by 2020)

E   S   P
0   25   55

---

tion

hly prized
g world,
ions and

' T-Shirt

T-shirt colors

? dispose / recycle

Story line:
Companies that invest in waste management projects in the developing world also benefit in global markets around carbon trading.

Related research studies:
New firm hopes to make Africa a hot carbon market ticket
+
CDMs Motivate New Waste Manage-ment Policies in Developing Countries

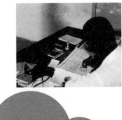

E   S   P
100   20   60

Tracing three sustainability factors through phases in the lifecycle(s), different scenarios were developed for T-shirts. A narrative was written based on related data, research and news reports. The story of this T-shirt extends over 30 years and thousands of kilometers, through pre- to post-consumption in the United States and Africa.

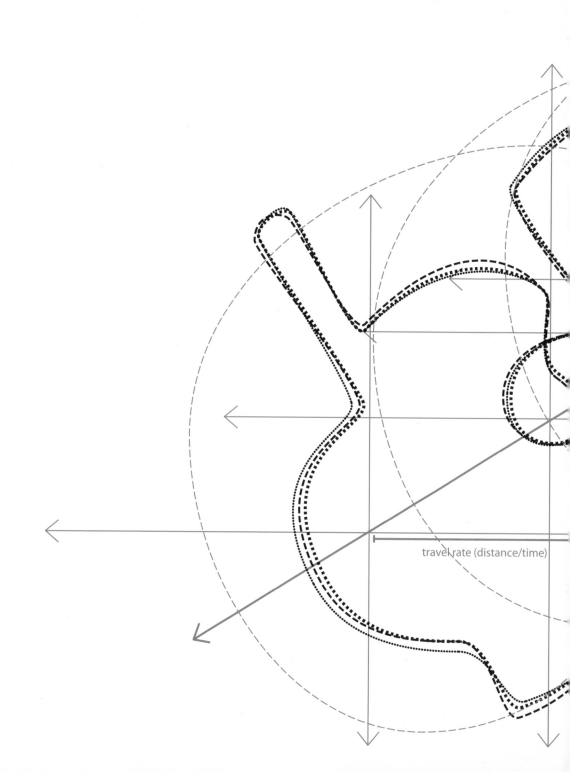

travel rate (distance/time)

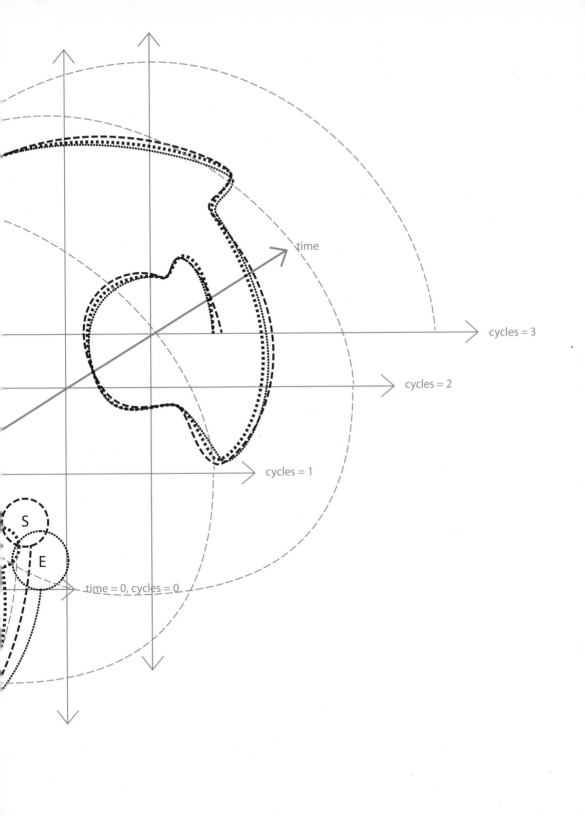

time

cycles = 3

cycles = 2

cycles = 1

S

E

time = 0, cycles = 0

Visualizing 3Ecologies

3Ecologies visualizes three sustainability factors at multiple key points throughout the extended lifecycle(s) of common products. While we have focused on one case study in order to develop the first prototype, the system is extensible to a wide variety of consumer goods. Future work includes the development of further cases and open-source mechanisms for adding cases to an expanding resource bank — this would enable close comparisons as well as broad overviews among products and product categories.

3Ecologies develops a complementary alternative to traditional approaches to lifecycle modeling. While these often reduce sustainability to data that can be directly measured, our approach emphasizes qualitative aspects and human factors and provides a dynamic and interactive experience of sustainability. Engaging in the complexity involved in lifecycle and sustainability models, users of 3Ecologies get personal and hands-on by tracing products through an vivid narrative and animated form. Interactive functions allow users to make choices, try out alternatives and trace potential consequences — aspects of presenting and learning about sustainability that are often left out of scientific data and economic predictions. 3Ecologies uses interactive visualization and immersive storytelling as the basis for an engaging experience of ecological thinking in action.

The information visualization, as prototyped, has been developed in terms of three modules that can be combined in different ways — the lifecycle(s) diagram, the 3Ecologies diagram and the product model. While the product modeled to date has been the case of the T-shirt, more cases of everyday products can be incorporated, brought to life through photo/video narratives.

Lifecycle(s) diagram

This module traces one or more lifecycles of a particular product through phases including agriculture, manufacture, retail, consumption, etc. Key points mark divergent paths effected by the decisions of actors involved — through the system, users can trace potential futures and consequences of these decisions.

3Ecologies diagram

Proportions among environmental, sociological, and psychological components of the diagram alter throughout the product lifecycle(s). This reflects the relative influence of each factor at different phases as well as the impact of users' decisions. This module is realized in two and three dimensions.

Product model

The system generates a model of the sustainability profile of a product over time. This integrates the lifecycle(s) and 3Ecologies diagrams, generating a unique model for users in real-time. This can be stored in a resource bank — other users can invesigate the data and decisions behind the model, as well as compare the consequences of alternative decisions or the profiles of other products and product categories.

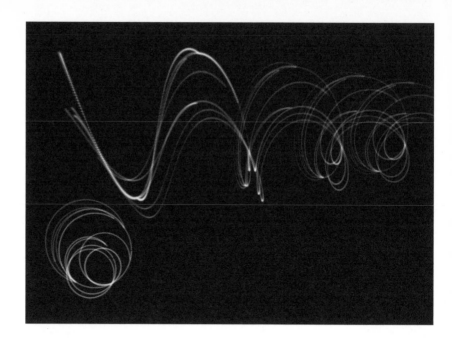

Lifecycle(s) diagram

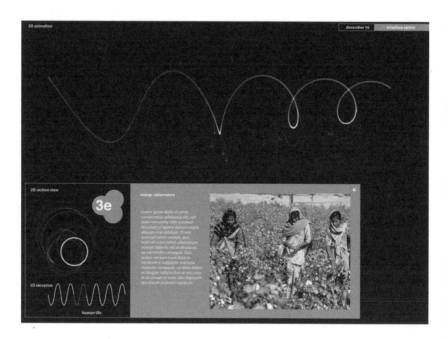

3Ecologies diagram

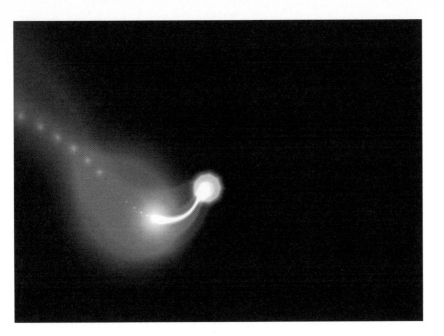

Product model

The product model (above), based on the T-shirt case, traces the shirt's trajectory over time and space through its multiple lifecycles. The sequence of images (next page) breaks down the product model into its parts and relations between the parts over time. Each circle represents one of the three ecologies (psychological, sociological or environmental). Each is assigned a color and diameter, based on the T-shirt case. In the product model (above), these are resolved into an animated and aesthetic form, which is 'incorporeal' and has multiple 'intensities', reflecting the dynamics of ecological complexity. Overlaps among the three colored circles (RGB) creates white, thus highlighting the idea of intensity and mutual influence.

Applying visualizations

As we have continued to develop 3Ecologies, we propose that the visualization could take multiple forms. To further develop these, we are seeking collaborators for future work, including environmental agencies, cultural institutions and design-oriented companies. Target audiences include industries and organizations involved in product research and development, scientific and design research communities and, importantly, the general public. Three possible forms are suggested, which can also be seen as proposals for future work.

As an open-source internet application, 3Ecologies could be developed as a knowledge platform for and by the design community. Users could upload data about products or product categories to a website, thereby generating visual models that could be compared, annotated and commented. Mechanisms for zooming and highlighting could support navigation at multiple scales and viewing products through alternative lenses.

3Ecologies could take the form of a graphic system for (future) eco-labeling retail products in stores. Options for consumers after point-of-purchase are presented via an attached tag, through simple 'what if' scenarios and graphics, based on the colour-coding and visual proportions of the three ecologies.

As an interactive museum installation, 3Ecologies could become a tool for the general public to 'try on' the consequences of their choices. An audio-visual animation, populated with rich stories from documentary sources, is the context for a visitor to experience the history of a familiar product and to make decisions that enact possible futures.

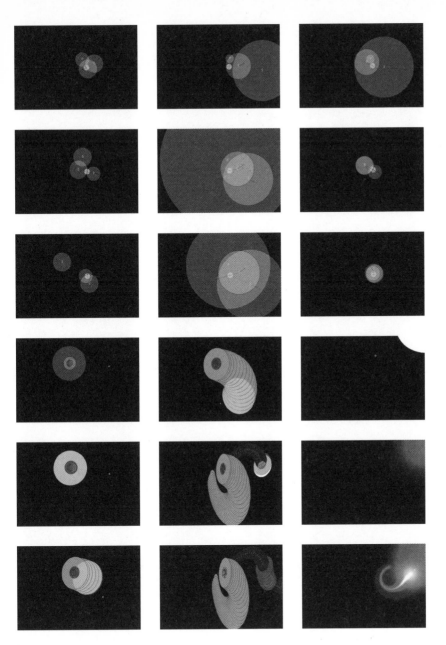

Product model

3Ecologies

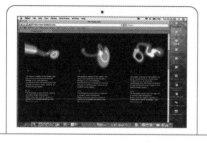

Open-source internet application

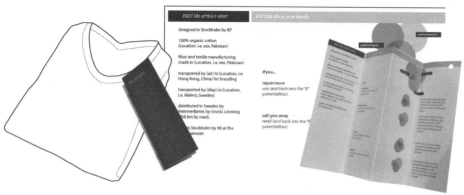

Product labeling system

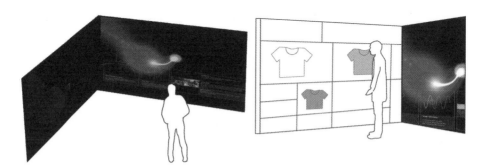

Interactive museum installation

Open-source internet application
A visualization of the 3Ecologies model would be generated case-by-case based on the events, occurrences and accidents in the life of an everyday product. In this way, visual comparisons can be made between different ways of producing/consuming the same product or between different kinds of products.

Product labeling system
Supplementing existing eco-labeling schemes, this would focus on the future life of a product. Summarizing the past life of a product, the "FUTURE LIFE in your hands" communicates the consequences "If you..." throw away, recycle, give away, etc., the product in the future.

Interactive museum installation
As a stand-alone exhibit or as a supplement to an existing design/architectural exhibition, this would be an immersive experience for hands-on engagement with ecological thinking in action. Visitors enact and view production/consumption choices by moving through and making selections within the exhibit.

3Ecologies has been sponsored through Iaspis, which is part of the Swedish Arts Grants Committee (Konstnärsnämden), and through Switch!, a design research program at the Interactive Institute sponsored by the Swedish Energy Agency.

Project team Martin Avila, John Carpenter, Ramia Mazé

Further reading A version of this text was previously and originally published as Martin Avila, John Carpenter and Ramia Mazé, "3Ecologies: Visualizing sustainability factors and futures," in *Proceedings of the LeNS Conference* (Sheffield, UK: Greenleaf, 2010): 382–395.

Green Memes

Tobi Schneidler, Tom Ballhatchet,
Solon Sasson (maoworks) with Ramia Mazé

'Green Memes' proposes an online social network and local kiosks for people to learn about energy consumption. Based on electricity data collected from smart grids, meters and sensors, data visualizations depict consumption per building, per person and at many other scales. A social networking function is attached to these — text messages, or 'green memes', invite users to engage with energy-savings advice, current events and sustainability research. Accessible online, through mobile devices, or installed locally, Green Memes combines 'hard data' with the 'soft power' of personalized information, public opinion and face-to-face communication. The project is currently seeking partners to further develop the system and interface design.

Communicating scales of energy use

Approaches to sustainable behavior often try to connect local actions to global change. In this project, we were interested in relating to a variety of scales in between the local and the global — sites and situations in which design might make new connections between these extremes. Desk → department → building → corporation → neighborhood → city → region → nation → planet — even throughout an ordinary work day, energy use takes place at many scales, with different possibilities for awareness, control and change.

Our initial research considered these different scales and respective systems connected to energy use. On one hand, there are social systems — conversations, interactions and media channels that effect personal beliefs and (sub) cultural trends. On the other hand, there are a range of current and near-future technical systems. For example, 'smart meters' enable power companies to automatically and remotely monitor data about electricity use in buildings and neighborhoods. 'Smart grids' not only monitor but negotiate and prioritize different demands placed on the grid, incorporating feedback mechanisms into system performance over time.

We were interested in the potential for feedback mechanisms that might allow energy users to have better information about their habits and choices — and to input information and ideas that might feed back into larger socio-technical processes. Perhaps smart technical networks for electricity monitoring and management might be overlaid with increasingly smart social networks concerned with energy use.

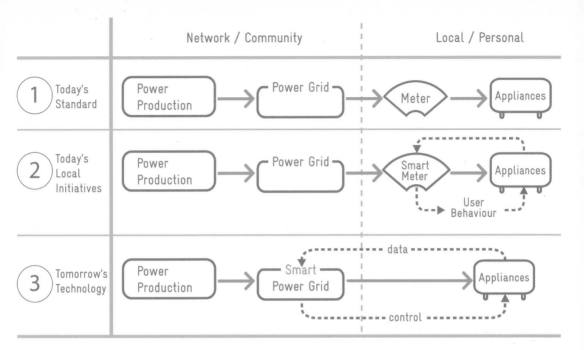

Network / Community   Local / Personal

(1) Today's Standard

Power Production → Power Grid → Meter → Appliances

(2) Today's Local Initiatives

Power Production → Power Grid → Smart Meter → Appliances

User Behaviour

(3) Tomorrow's Technology

Power Production → Smart Power Grid → Appliances

data

control

(4) Proposal for Green Meme Machine

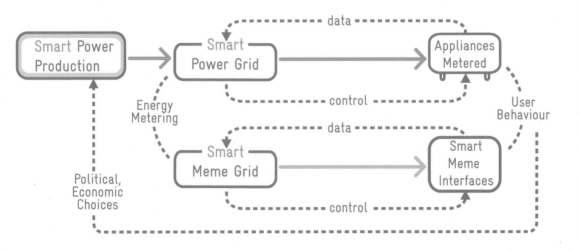

Smart Power Production → Smart Power Grid → Appliances Metered

Energy Metering

data

control

User Behaviour

Political, Economic Choices

Smart Meme Grid → Smart Meme Interfaces

data

control

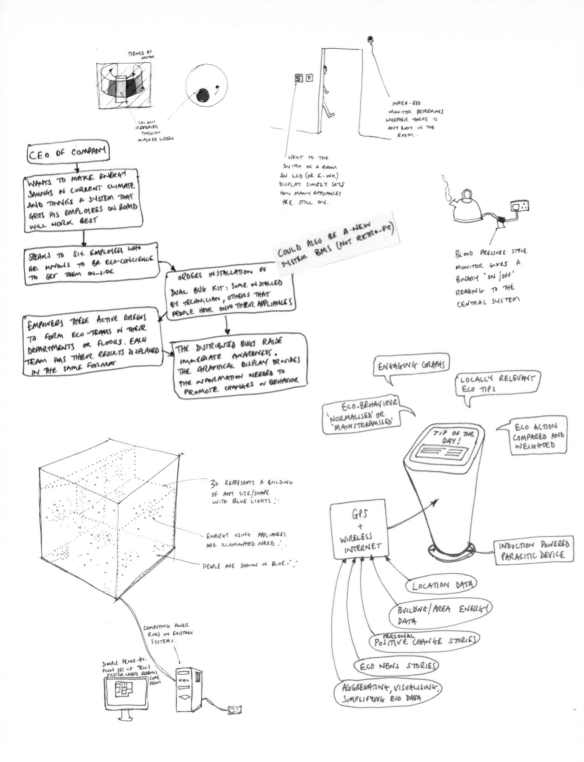

TURNED BY MOTOR

COLOUR REVEALED THROUGH MASKED SCREEN

INFRA-RED MONITOR DETERMINES WHETHER THERE IS ANY BODY IN THE ROOM.

NEXT TO THE SWITCH IN A ROOM AN LCD (OR E-INK) DISPLAY SIMPLY SAYS HOW MANY APPLIANCES ARE STILL ON.

BLOOD PRESSURE STYLE MONITOR GIVES A BINARY 'ON/OFF' READING TO THE CENTRAL SYSTEM

CEO OF COMPANY

WANTS TO MAKE ENERGY SAVINGS IN CURRENT CLIMATE AND THINKS A SYSTEM THAT GETS HIS EMPLOYEES ON BOARD WILL WORK BEST

SPEAKS TO SIX EMPLOYEES WHO HE KNOWS TO BE ECO-CONSCIENCE TO GET THEM ON-SIDE

EMPOWERS THESE ACTIVE GREENS TO FORM ECO-TEAMS IN THEIR DEPARTMENTS OR FLOORS. EACH TEAM HAS THEIR RESULTS DISPLAYED IN THE SAME FORMAT

ORDERS INSTALLATION OF DUAL BUG KIT: SOME INSTALLED BY TECHNICIAN, OTHERS THAT PEOPLE HOOK ONTO THEIR APPLIANCES

COULD ALSO BE A NEW SYSTEM BMS (NOT RETRO-FIT)

THE DISTRIBUTED BUGS RAISE IMMEDIATE AWARENESS. THE GRAPHICAL DISPLAY PROVIDES THE INFORMATION NEEDED TO PROMOTE CHANGES IN BEHAVIOR

ENGAGING GRAPHS

LOCALLY RELEVANT ECO TIPS

ECO-BEHAVIOUR 'NORMALISED' OR 'MAINSTREAMISED'

TIP OF THE DAY!

ECO ACTION COMPARED AND WEIGHTED

3D REPRESENTS A BUILDING OF ANY SIZE/SHAPE WITH BLUE LIGHTS

ENERGY USING APPLIANCES ARE ILLUMINATED IN RED

PEOPLE ARE SHOWN IN BLUE

GPS + WIRELESS INTERNET

INDUCTION POWERED PARASITIC DEVICE

LOCATION DATA

BUILDING/AREA ENERGY DATA

PERSONAL POSITIVE CHANGE STORIES

ECO NEWS STORIES

AGGREGATING, VISUALISING, SIMPLIFYING ECO DATA

COMPUTING POWER RUNS ON EXISTING SYSTEMS.

SIMPLE FLOOR-BY-FLOOR SET UP TELLS SYSTEM WHERE READINGS CAME FROM

Switch!

We began imagining new (and interdisciplinary) connections between social and technical systems. In the field of architectural engineering, buildings are increasing designed or retrofitted with technologies that sense energy and climate factors. In the area of information technology and interaction design, online social networking tools and semantic web techniques connect interest groups and communities. We imagined combinations of off-the-shelf and emerging technologies integrated into the built environment for making information about energy visible and tangible. Early sketches included: Do-It-Yourself kits for tapping into data flows, eco-labeling buildings and 2-, 3- and 4-dimensional displays.

Two design principles became increasingly important as different concepts were sketched, discussed, revised, critiqued and compared. For one thing, we began to focus on the individual as the primary unit for measuring and displaying data. In this way, a potentially overwhelming amount of data about electricity would always be aggregated and represented in ways that relate to a person's realm of perception and influence. Secondly, we increasingly noticed the power of people's 'personal change stories' to influence others. This is evident in proliferating social and advisory services around sustainability and in rapid behavioral changes effected when tipping points in fuel costs are exceeded.

Taking on these two principles enabled us to connect the personal and community scale — exploring a range of one-to-one, one-to-many, many-to-many and many-to-one communications and interactions. We began to develop design concepts that would build up from the local into a more global effect, that might involve different peer groups, and that might tricke down from larger to smaller spheres of influence.

Designing a (social) network system

'Memes' are ideas or behaviors that can pass from one person to another through the social sphere. The term was introduced in 1976 by the biologist Richard Dawkins to describe social phenomena that follow the same principle in society as genes do in biology. Like genes, memes are copied with variation and selection, they are reproduced and propagated, starting with individual instances and growing in society by survival of the fittest.

During design development of the project, we connected to the concept and the function of memes in order to relate to the ways that personal experiences and success stories can be spread among peers and communities. We were interested in how people's ideas about sustainability — 'green memes' — could be expressed and discussed through the design of a social network present in everyday places and devices.

We developed a concept for a social networking system — the Green Meme Machine — which would mix 'hard data' about energy use with the 'soft power' of input by energy users, effectively building a smart social network on top of a smart electricity grid. In our concept, quantitative data about the electricity consumption of an individual person or building is visualized as statistics. In addition to this data visualization, the system makes use of these visuals to provide occasions for social interaction. As they view the statistics, individuals would be able to browse and input short text statements about energy and sustainability, which would then circulate publicly as topics for discussion and debate.

Green Memes would exist within the system as short statements, or text messages. As viewed or voted on by others, they would grow and spread or, conversely, shrink and disappear. The interface is designed to express the flow of memes bubbling up, connecting with others, spreading and evolving over time.

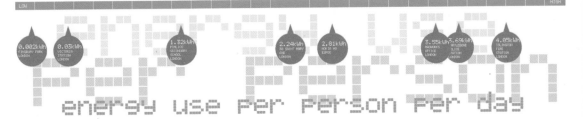

energy use per person per day

- 0.002kWh FINSBURY PARK LONDON
- 0.03kWh VICTORIA STATION LONDON
- 1.32kWh PUBLIC SECONDARY SCHOOL LONDON
- 2.24kWh 100 SAINT MARY AXE LONDON
- 2.81kWh NOKIA HQ ESPOO
- 3.55kWh HACKNEY OFFICE LONDON
- 3.69kWh APPLEDORE SLICE JAPAN
- 4.05kWh ISLINGTON FIRE STATION LONDON

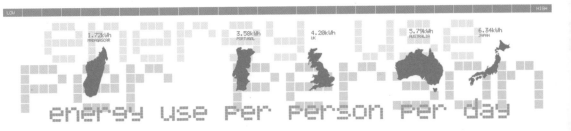

energy use per person per day

- 1.72kWh MADAGASCAR
- 3.58kWh PORTUGAL
- 4.20kWh UK
- 5.79kWh AUSTRALIA
- 6.34kWh JAPAN

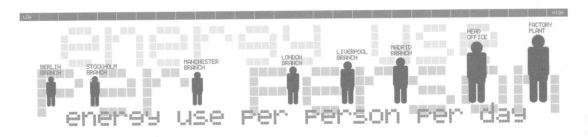

energy use per person per day

- BERLIN BRANCH
- STOCKHOLM BRANCH
- MANCHESTER BRANCH
- LONDON BRANCH
- LIVERPOOL BRANCH
- MADRID BRANCH
- HEAD OFFICE
- FACTORY PLANT

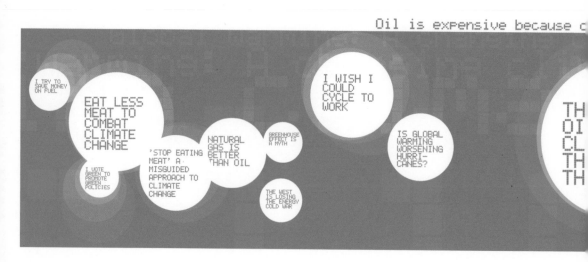

I TRY TO
SAVE MONEY
ON FUEL

EAT LESS
MEAT TO
COMBAT
CLIMATE
CHANGE

'STOP EATING
MEAT' A
MISGUIDED
APPROACH TO
CLIMATE
CHANGE

NATURAL
GAS IS
BETTER
THAN OIL

GREENHOUSE
EFFECT IS
A MYTH

I VOTE
GREEN TO
PROMOTE
GREEN
POLICIES

THE WEST
IS LOSING
THE ENERGY
COLD WAR

I WISH I
COULD
CYCLE TO
WORK

IS GLOBAL
WARMING
WORSENING
HURRI-
CANES?

TH
OI
CL
TH
TH

Switch!

OF

U

I WISH IO
COULD USE
MY CAR
LESS

HYBRID CARS
ARE NO
BETTER THAN
INTELLIGENT
'RS

I SIGNED A
NO-FLY
PLEDGE

EXTREME + RISKY
ACTION THE ONLY
WAY TO TACKLE
GLOBAL WARMING

PLASTIC
BAGS ARE
KILLING
US

CONCENTRAT-
ING ON
SOLAR POWER
BETTER
OPTION THAN
NUCLEAR
POWER

GLOBAL
WARMING IS
NOT REALLY
HAPPENING

SAVING THE
PLANET
BEGINS AT
HOME

BOUGHT
BEAN
'ON
'DITS

GREEN
YOUR
SEX
LIFE

NATURAL
GAS IS
BETTER
THAN OIL

WE DO NOT
NEED
NUCLEAR
POWER

91

Green Memes

The Green Meme Machine would be global (as an internet-enabled software program) but would come to life locally. Through internet-enabled functions on mobile phones or personal computers, people would be able to input, read and interact with ideas circulated through the Green Meme Machine.

Further, we propose a kiosk version that could be commissioned by a corporation or public organization to be stationed in their lobby, atrium or plaza for a period of time. This version would take particular advantage of the locale — connecting directly to local electricity metering and potentially to the kinds of sensor networks and automation systems that are increasingly designed or retrofit into buildings. This would enable more extensive and detailed data to be gathered, based not only on the building as a whole, but also floors, sections and rooms.

Kiosks located in multiple buildings, such as branches of an organization in different cities or countries, could also build up a 'trans-local' network. Site-specific data and interactions could be built not only within, but across, locations. Additional functionality would include mechanisms for collaboration as well as competition among peers and groups and debates about energy issues in different geographic conditions and cultures. Potentially associated with a social responsibility campaign within the organization, the kiosk could function as a vehicle for catalyzing and supporting sustainable initiatives on an individual, local and trans-local basis.

Interacting with Green Memes

The Green Meme Machine consists of an IT system and software interface that enables people to interact with information about their personal energy consumption and with a world of data and ideas about sustainability. To relate to different scales of activity and information systems, the proposal includes online, mobile and fixed access- and touch-points. Keepsakes, such as personalized screensavers can be downloaded, and bumper stickers and badges printed, as 'take-home' formats. Through interactive and analog media, the Green Meme Machine is extended as a platform for further offline and face-to-face interactions. It exists as — an urban presence → online presence → mobile presence → graphic presence. Touchpoints are designed for various levels of use and types of users — the kiosk for a local community, badges for the casual user and online functions for budding activists.

The system depends upon a diversity of positions expressed by individuals and the participation of a critical mass of participants acting in multiple locations. An antidote to green preaching and top-down social responsibility programs, this system is constituted and sustained by the participation of many, leveraging motivations ranging from self-expression and personal research, to group bonding and peer pressure. This also suggests the possibility for creating further feedback loops — among colleagues on coffee breaks, between employees and employers, between stakeholders and energy providers.

The project appeals to corporate social responsibility — after all, corporations and other large organizations can have a unique role in hosting both a local and a global conversation around sustainability. Since individuals and nation-states are bound to a particular scale of action of scope of concern, there is a vacuum of power with respect

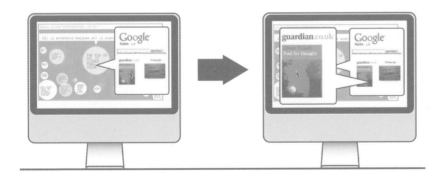

Green Memes

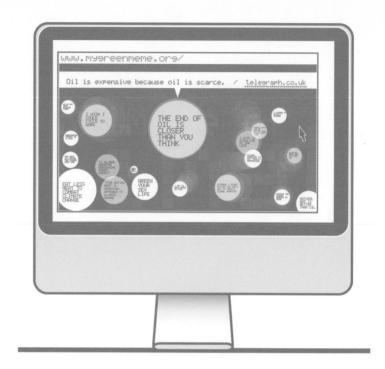

to environmental issues, providing an opportunity for other entities to become powerful social actors.

To explain how Green Memes might be experienced by users in everyday life, we developed a scenario. While this scenario is envisioned for a large-scale implementation of the project, we also have versions for small-scale events and low-cost tests.

We start the story in the headquarters of a large corporation, which has developed a collaboration with an independent and trusted NGO (non-governmental organization) to commission the Green Meme Machine kiosk for their lobby during several months. On first encounter, an employee or passer-by would see the kiosk, which is made of a surface that doubles as a screen and curves to provide an enclosed space for viewing, interacting and meeting. The screen displays bubbles of different sizes displaying text messages that are animated — growing and shrinking, these statements invite them to further explore the information and people behind these memes by stepping into the kiosk.

Venturing inside, the inner surface of the kiosk displays further information, as a series of graphical visualizations. The default visualization and starting point for the user is information about energy consumption — this can be displayed per country, building, floor, business unit, etc. In the middle of the kiosk, there is a mechanism for scrolling and comparing different sets of data. The numbers are always based on a 'per person' average, taking a human-scale and user-centered view upon sets and scales of data.

Some memes are positive, some are negative... and some are just strange. This appeals to one user portrayed in our scenario. He is skeptical when companies use 'green wash' to sell products. *Why is the Manchester office using less electricity than us here?*, he wonders. *It's a complex issue,* says a passing colleague. *Is Manchester performing better than us?* He responds, *No idea, but we can ask Susan — she was working up there not long ago.*

The kiosk also contains a badge vending machine — a favorite meme can be selected and printed — and worn as a public statement. By making a selection, the user has 'adopted a meme' which also gives it further life within the online system. The badge displays a URL — through the web browser of a computer or mobile phone, users can explore the meme in more depth and input their own memes into the system. In the browser interface to the Green Meme Machine, each bubble links to further information — selecting the text bubble opens up a range of related and constantly updated stories collected from leading news and research organizations. The technical system generating these links is based on keywords extracted and searched through the existing online system for Google News. This stream of information unfolds diverse perspectives and positions in relation to the topic of the meme.

"The 'end of oil' is closer than you think"
> Oil Futures, Focus On Energy Information Administration. Wall Street Journal, 6 hours ago > Book Review: The End of Oil, by Paul Roberts. Guardian.co.uk, April 2006 > Energy Survivalists Prepare for End of Oil-fired Economy. Seattle Times, May 2008 > The End of Oil? Breakthrough Turns Coal Into Clean Diesel. National Geographic, April 2006 > US and China Slipping Into a Conflict Over Oil. Arab News, July 2005 > Reporting Oil Reserves is a Political Act. Hindu Business Line, Nov 2006 >

Browsing these exposes different viewpoints, providing a more in-depth view of a topic and a basis for users to take their own position on the topic. By emphasizing multiple and contrasting viewpoints, as well as the development of the discourse and knowledge over time, the system embodies the fact that there is no single truth nor complete solution to complex issues such as climate change. Nonetheless, the system provides resources for users to become better informed, to articulate their own position, and to engage with others.

Communication and interaction technologies are integrated as instruments for people to conduct their own investigation of the topics at hand. The system integrates data about energy as well as the reported status of scientific knowledge and technology development — but it also emphasizes the socio-cultural context in which this information is received by individuals and related to other sorts and sources of information. Enriching facts about energy use, the system links people into a wider network of other energy users and world of opinions about sustainability.

Green Memes is part of Switch!, a design research program at the Interactive Institute sponsored by the Swedish Energy Agency.

Project team Ramia Mazé (Interactive Institute) and Tobi Schneidler, Tom Ballhatchet, Solon Sasson (maoworks). The maoworks design agency has been commissioned for the project, which has been developed as a collaboration.

Telltale

Jenny Bergström, Brendon Clark,
Alberto Frigo, Ramia Mazé,
Johan Redström, Anna Vallgårda

'Telltale' is a piece of furniture that collects traces of energy (mis)use. Connected remotely to a household's electricity meter, it responds to increases or decreases in energy consumption. Increases cause its internal structure to become less robust and, when used in weakened states, its textile surface becomes prone to flaking, crackling and wrinkling. Telltale decomposes more or less quickly — users participate in the (de)formation of an object that tells them about themselves, others and the cumulative effect of local actions. A prototype has been built and studied within two households — alterations in household actions as well as family interactions were prompted by Telltale, evolving as the object changed over time in use.

Experimenting with materials

Telltale stems from a discussion around sustainability issues such as private ownership, planned obsolescence and fuel dependency. In particular, we were interested in the increasing use of electricity in an expanding range of everyday things that we have come to depend upon. Electricity fuels functions basic to survival, to social structures and personal identity. Despite our increasing dependency, however, the status of electricity in the home is typically present only through an electric meter hidden away in the basement or periodic energy bills presented to the head of household for payment. Telltale is an inquiry into alternative expressions of energy consumption, an aesthetics imbedded in intimate domestic space and entangled in everyday family life.

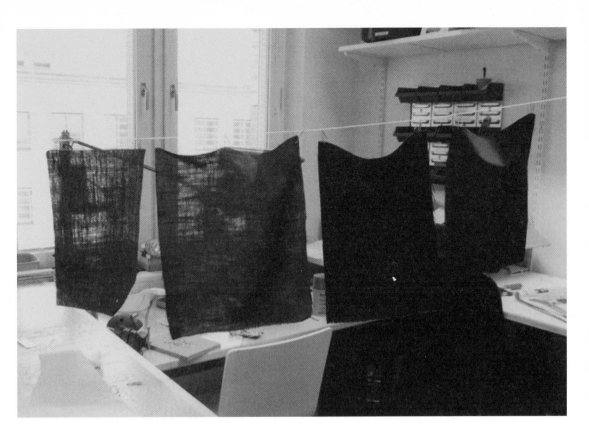

This builds on our previous research in textile design
— specifically, in (inter)active materials made possible
with the integration of computational and mechanical
technologies. Embedded sensors, for example, mean that
surface appearance or physical structure can be made to
respond to external conditions such as climate and use.
Further, inbuilt memory entails that sensed conditions can
be collected and expressed in the material over time. Such
extensions of traditional and familiar materials open up
for new ways of thinking about the intersection between
technical systems and material culture.

In Telltale, we took the potentials of smart textiles
as a basis for rethinking the material expressions of energy
consumption patterns. Aesthetic inspiration came from

the material culture of wear and aging and from ecological concepts of lifecycles and resilience.

Starting with the existing material culture of the home, we considered the expressiveness of textile furnishings. Any such material, given time, will reflect its context, use and users through natural disintegration, deformation and patina — aesthetic qualities that may also be associated with personal memories and family events. In addition to the physics and chemistry behind such properties of materials, integrated computation increases the potential for cause-and-effect reactions to (or interactions with) the local environment.

These properties entail that materials continue to change — or become — over time. Factors such as climate and use may change the material through direct contact and through data sensed and collected, which can be used to modulate or modify the material. It also means that users can have an even more substantial impact on material expressions, since it is not only their direct actions that affect the material, but also the effects of data collected, centralized and stored about their actions and behaviors.

To explore a range of material expressions of change over time, we created a set of more than twenty textile samples. Each was approximately the same size, but with different material components and finishes. We also varied the number and duration of applied surface treatments, which had an effect on how brittle, durable or bonded the composite would become after setting and drying.

Handling these materials allowed us to experiment with various changing expressions, some of which would be able to change back to an original state, or switch between different states, while others would be aggregate, permanent and irreversible. Subjecting the samples to various abrasions, we were able to anticipate the impacts and processes that the material might undergo in future contexts of use.

We also realized that expressions would be dependant upon the construction and orientation of the material in a use context. As textile is applied to a piece of furniture, for example, aspects of wear-and-tear appear differently where there is direct contact. Further, discrete structural changes affect the seams and corners where multiple surfaces are joined. In order to explore these variables, we constructed a full-scale, 3-dimensional material sample. Though it did not have a stable inner structure able to support body weight, we simulated the effects of a human body in terms of size, orientation and movement.

Through this hands-on and collaborative experimentation, we sketched out possible material expressions considering visual and structural aspects as well as temporal variables in the material's performance and deformation over time.

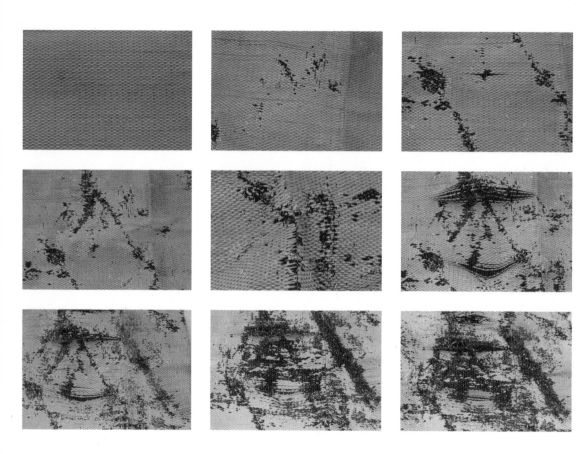

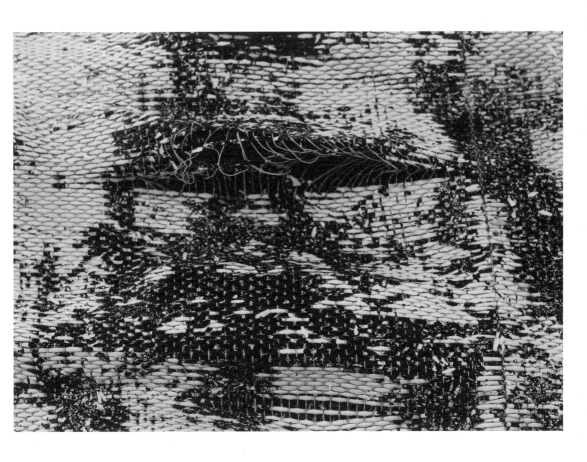

Telltale

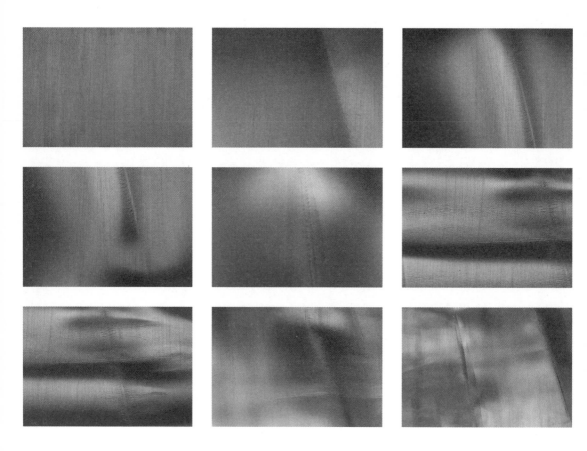

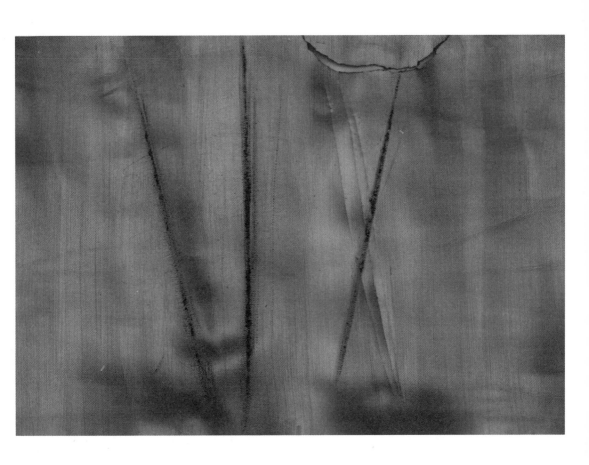

Telltale

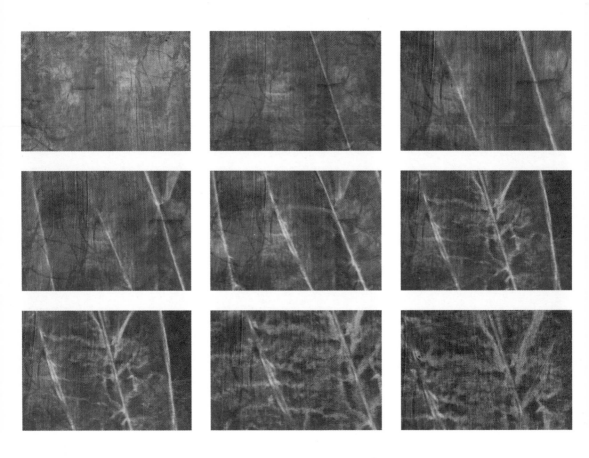

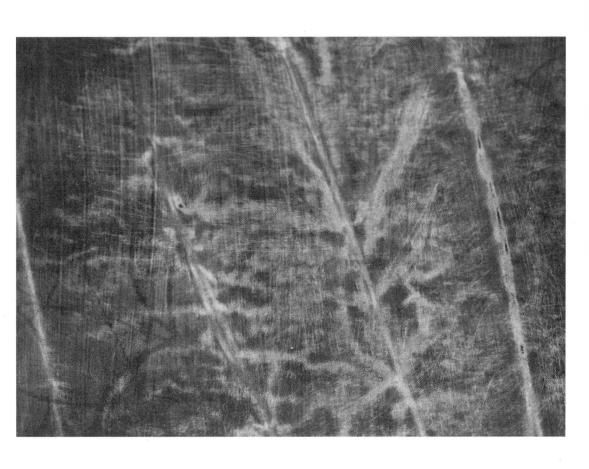

Telltale

Crafting a transitional object

Another starting point included current approaches to treating dependence on energy in terms of addiction. We were inspired by the psychological theory of 'transitional objects', which accompany people from one stage in life to another, and related theories within material culture studies that examine the material basis for expressing identity and shaping social relations.

An example noted for its role in emotional and social development is a child's comfort blanket. Often hand-made or woven from textiles and given as a gift, it evades typical conceptions of design products. As a gift, for instance, its value lies outside the terms of industrial mass production and market consumption. It has a fragile and intimate materiality, placed close to the body at a time of transition to a more personal conception of self, sometimes with ritualistic or fetishistic connotations. A personal and cultural — but ephemeral — object, it either disintegrates or outlives its purpose in time.

Inspired by aspects of such transitional objects, Telltale has been developed in terms of a particular set of aesthetic qualities as well as a mechanism for transition. Gradually collecting traces of use, it expresses and signals domestic energy consumption within family life. In time, decisions and behaviors around energy consumption might take place more explicitly and through other products — Telltale marks the subtle transition from the invisibility to an increasing awareness of electricity. After such a transition takes place in one household, it circulates to another. Travelling from house to house, it communicates locally, to its immediate users, and carries traces of those who came before.

Telltale initially appears as a generic form, with a neutral color and shape that might suit any range of spaces or functions. Over time, in use, the surface and shape of Telltale design evolve along two temporal scales.

One is deliberately slow, a visual pattern within an analog and familiar material. People sit on Telltale, use it as a footstool, place other things on top. Over time, ordinary wear-and-tear builds into a pattern that is slightly organic or even geographic in appearance, in a secondary color within the material that is revealed as it cracks or wears thin. This gives an appearance not only of disintegration but of overall transformation.

The second is a more immediate response to daily use of energy within the context of the home, based on data collected from the household electricity meter. This is expressed as a change in the mechanical properties of Telltale — energy consumption affects the more (or less) stable internal structure of the furniture and, thus, functionality for everyday activities such as sitting. As Telltale is used in weakened states, when increasing energy consumption has caused its internal structure to become less stable or robust, its textile surface becomes more prone to flaking, crackling and wrinkling.

The first, slow transformation depends upon the second, immediate structural condition and real-time use. Telltale, thus, expresses local acts of energy consumption as well as a longer trends and patterns. The expression of the object is built up locally and accumulated across multiple households. Over time, the aesthetic of each Telltale becomes unique, a joint product of energy consumption and daily use — the object becomes an increasingly valuable record of domestic life, even as its durability is made more precarious due to increased dependency on personal actions and collective effort.

Prototyping expressions of energy

While much research in the area of new materials is driven by technology development, our concern in Telltale has focused on the expressions and effects of materials in relation to everyday life and lifestyles. This has meant that we have had to develop working methods for driving the research forward in terms of other values — in particular, we have oriented our process around aesthetic and social questions in order to explore aspects of perception, experience and use from the start.

An important consideration has been the development of methods for design-driven material research. Of course, this is not unprecedented — there is a long history of material innovation and materials science driven by the empirical experimentation of artists, artisans and designers. Over the centuries, for example, ironmongers and jewelers have developed hands-on techniques (such as sequences of heating, annealing, quenching and hammering) to manipulate complex properties of metal that could not even be explained by science until recently.

Before we made technology and design decisions in Telltale, we experimented with material properties and expressions over time, in multiple contexts. The textile samples exemplify how we developed working methods for exploring aesthetic possibilities. We recognized that the aesthetics were dependant upon context and also upon use — and thus hinged upon social questions.

We decided to develop a prototype to be deployed into households for gaining a better understanding of both the possible material expressions of Telltale and the potential effects in use and on users. Technically, this entailed a shift from focusing only on the surface effects to structure and shape. While we maintained our premise in the potentials of high-tech and smart materials, we developed a version with low-tech methods for rapidly prototyping the basic concept. This reflects our intention to engage use and

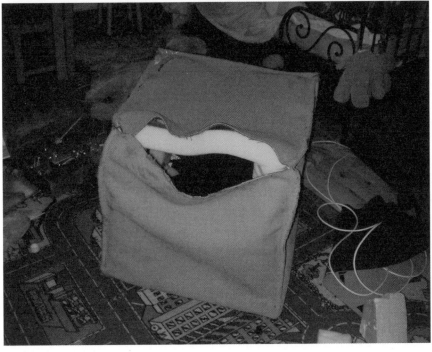

users early within a design-driven process, before decisions about any ideal or final technology were set.

We sketched construction techniques for the prototype that simulated the mechanical and computational performances of possible material composites. One was based on a structure that would rise and fall in discrete, geometric sections, and another was based on a more fluid inflation and collapse. Rough prototypes were made borrowing on the structural principle of 'tensegrity'.

Based on this principle and early models, a full-scale prototype was constructed. The rigid armatures of the models were replaced with pliable reinforcements inserted into the seams and corners. The prototype was stabilized by a weighted base. Change in the form over time was achieved through inflation and deflation of the airtight material construction, complemented with other soft and elastic components built in.

The prototype simulated certain surface and structural properties that might achieved with high-tech composites of new materials. Many new materials integrate complex (inter)active properties that present challenges for designers with respect to discovering, working with and exploiting the potentials of new materials. Within design practice, this has entailed the development of methods for mocking-up and testing out potential design directions.

For experimental purposes in Telltale, our development of a low-tech and low-fidelity prototype with basic construction techniques and off-the-shelf components enabled us to try out aesthetic and experiential variables at full-scale. Early on, we could explore various effects 'in the field' and over time. Within a design-driven process, we crafted diverse, complex and emergent material expressions — and, in the next phase of the project, extended these outside the research lab and design studio into situations of use.

The Telltale prototype was developed in order to gather initial insights into how such an object might prompt reflection on domestic energy consumption. Specifically, we wanted to investigate how its changing material and formal expression might occasion interpretations and interactions within daily family life over time.

An initial study of the prototype was conducted with the participation of two families in Stockholm over three weeks. One was a family of four, including two children, visiting the city and staying in a borrowed apartment with Telltale for ten days. The other was the young couple who owned the apartment, who were away on holiday during the family's visit and returned to find Telltale in their home. While investigation of shared product ownership was not the purpose of this study, selection of a visiting and a permanent family allowed us to probe into some issues about products as temporary or new, chosen or prescribed, strange or familiar.

The experimental design process in Telltale entailed the development of research methods grounded in an aesthetics of materials and use. To conduct the study, we defined a series of manual adjustments to the shape of the prototype — four form adjustments to Telltale were made by a researcher during the family stay, for example. These were based on energy consumption recorded by the electricity meter before, during and after Telltale use. By manually exaggerating changes in the prototype, the study accelerated a process in which insights were gathered.

The study also entailed the development of methods for exploring the interaction between aesthetic and social questions. Led by a design anthropologist, the study has been conducted as a sort of 'performative ethnography'. This involves traditional methods of observation and, as an important complement, activities in which the researcher and the families participate together in discussions about and activities around Telltale. This took place as two sit-down interviews with the family, observations during their stay and casual conversations. The owners were interviewed once, two days after their return. Crafting and staging occasions around Telltale, the researcher is an integrated part of the social dynamic and actively generates a reflective and discursive context during the study.

The focus of the study was to see what verbal and non-verbal 'expressions of awareness' would be occasioned by the prototype and by the activity of the study itself. Overall, the Telltale inquiry provoked the participants to:
— Express and practice their understanding of energy consumption
— Create links between behavior of artifact and behavior of people
— Express and reinforce aesthetic preferences
— Educate each other about energy consumption
— Opine and defend their own energy-related practices
In this case, we were not studying what 'real' use might be like nor how 'real' users might change their energy behaviors — these are goals typical in usability or other studies of near-final product prototypes. Instead, Telltale acted as a catalyst for observing and discussing the materiality of electricity in everyday life.

Reflecting on Telltale expressions

The surface and shape of Telltale are crafted so that they might be transformed long after design — within particular contexts of use over time. In response to household use of energy and use as furniture, it collects traces of consumption practices in the home. The expression and experience of a seemingly ordinary design product become dependent upon — and reflective of — another (but often invisible) type of consumption. The evolving surface pattern and structural properties evoke an organic aesthetics that, amplifying ordinary wear-and-tear, eventually lead to disintegration.

While it does not function as a direct visualization of data or as an overtly pedagogical device, Telltale occasions another sort of reflection and conversation about consumption in the home. Refraining from merely applying aesthetics to make data more appealing or accessible, or from judging consumption in terms of simplistic categories of 'good' or 'bad', Telltale acts as a sort of *tabula rasa* upon which a variety of more complex and cumulative practices of consumption are traced. Just as there is no single or final answer to how people should live today, Telltale provides no singular message or final judgment about energy consumption.

Instead, the formation of the object's structure and aesthetics, as well as interpretations about what it might indicate in terms of behavior and meaning, are left deliberately open to debate. The study, for example, provided preliminary but valuable indications of how individuals and families might perceive and interpret the material expressions. In various ways, people reacted and adjusted their use of the object and their energy consumption in response. Telltale occasioned new conversations and interactions among family members upon their perceptions and behaviors around electricity in the home.

In response to issues around the private ownership and planned obsolescence of products, Telltale intervenes another point of view. The proposed circulation and exchange service means that it would respond to local use and accumulate traces of multiple users over time. Its form is not up to design — local and cumulative use determines its basic aesthetics. Nor are its accumulated aesthetics neutral — even as it gains increasingly meaningful traces, these are in the form of material disintegration. Its future becomes precarious due to its contingency upon current use. Further, collected traces become public property — shared ownership means that personal information shapes the form and fate of a collective product.

Deliberately countering conventional assumptions about consumer products and private data, as well as reversing the primacy of design and use in determining form, Telltale has been a platform for us to question relations between production and consumption. Both in terms of the form and the function of Telltale, questions of use have been central to conceptual and design development — to whether and how formation occurs. This reflects a proposition that sustainability can be achieved not (or not only) through new and improved technology nor by shaping human behavior through 'good' design — instead, sustainability emerges from complex practices of consumption within everyday social life. This prompts a range of new perspectives on design, including how materials and methods might open up for and occasion people's ongoing reflections. This points to a need for continuing experimentation with the aesthetics of materials and form — and new material practices of design and of use.

Telltale is part of Switch!, a design research program at the Interactive Institute sponsored by the Swedish Energy Agency, with additional funding from the Swedish Governmental Agency for Innovation Systems (VINNOVA) through the Smart Textiles Initiative.

Project team Jenny Bergström, Ramia Mazé, Johan Redström, Anna Vallgårda. The prototype was built with Alberto Frigo and the household study was led by Brendon Clark.

Thanks to the two families who participated in the household study.

Further reading A version of this text was previously and originally published as Jenny Bergström, Brendon Clark, Alberto Frigo, Ramia Mazé, Johan Redström and Anna Vallgårda, "Becoming Materials: Material forms and forms of practice," *Digital Creativity* 21, no. 3 (2010): 155–172.

Ab|Norm

**Loove Broms, Karin Ehrnberger,
Ramia Mazé**

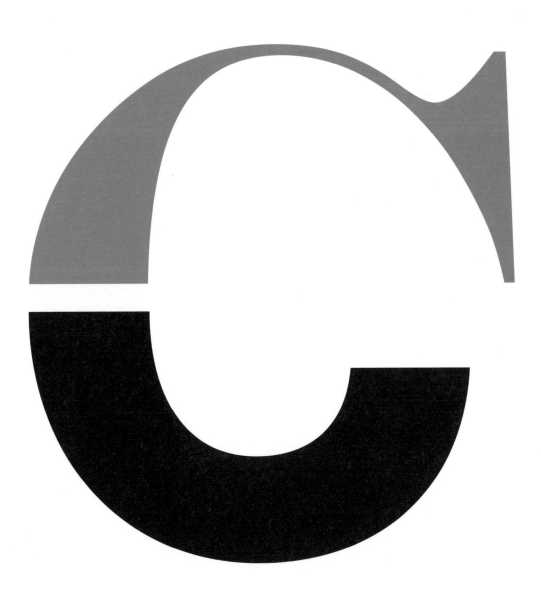

'AblNorm' inquires into the presence and use of energy in public. Many functions and forms of electricity have long been 'naturalized' into our habitual actions and cultural norms. Consider how the lighting in our streets and parks conditions what activities we can do and when, what a neighborhood identity is like or even how safe we feel. We may not always take notice of the electricity present — much less accompanying values and consequences. AblNorm sketches urban interventions in order to discuss such issues with stakeholders. A series of concept designs has been produced in the form of cards, which have already been the basis for a participatory workshop with architects, artists and engineers.

En vanlig dag i mitt liv...

Tänk på en typiskt vardaglig situation eller händelse i ditt vardagsliv som utspelar sig i offentlig miljö. Det kan t ex vara när du lämnar barn på dagis, besöker en vän eller söndagspromenaden. Försök återge denna händelse i tre steg, som en liten berättelse. Vilka detaljer är utmärkande för förloppet? Vilka är där? Vad händer runt omkring? Hur ser miljön ut?
Vilken känsla bär du med dig? Skriv stödord och rita gärna!

Resa till jobb

1 Väntar på bussen	2 Bussresa - h-holm hyrpla → Slussen	3 Promenad Slussen → jobb
klocka	Slussen Fasad	← kaffe
Väntar på buss vid k-holm kyrka	Om i sällskap i samtal	väljer oftast Götgatan
tittar efter hur många minuter	Annars sitter jag på hörser	istället för tre pporna
det är tills buss 3 går	Side av buss. Ser på miljön	upp till mosebacke.
Ser efter på lyktstolpet vad	Stadshuset riddarholmen	kanske träffar jag en
klockan är, vissa dagar	tegelbacken. Ser alltid på	vän, på I så fall uppe
sällskap med grannar eller	Slussen fasaden	upp för klevens gata
föräldrar på kannans skola	håller klockan på betivindrar	Går alltid mitt i gata,
Om buss eller jag är senstress	när jag är framme	inte trottoar, över
folk väntar. Barn går över	Andra på väg till jobb.	mosebacketorg, framme.
gata in h.a "trafikvärd"	Lastbilar med leverans öl mat	

En ovanlig dag i mitt liv...

Välj ut två av koncepten som ni tycker passar bäst in i era berättelser och skapa två nya berättelser utifrån dem. Rita kartor över platsen där berättelsen utspelar sig och placera in koncepten i dessa. Diskutera vad som händer och skriv ned stödord.

Att tänka på när ni diskuterar och utvärderar berättelserna:
Var är energi närvarande? Hur förändras berättelsen av konceptet? Hur påverkas platsen och människorna? Långsiktigt, kortsiktigt? Vilket budskap förmedlar konceptet?
Vad är bra och vad är dåligt? Vad är intressant och vad känns mest spännande med just detta koncept? Var är konceptet placerat och varför? Hur kan konceptet förändras för att bättre passa in i sammanhanget? Är det någon plats där konceptet bättre skulle passa in?

Glöm inte att motivera valet av berättelse!

+ Bra utblick

Kontorstryck implementeras i ett område hos hammarbygötland.

På längsikt i flera innedelar. Kan man jämföra olika
områden?

Ett bra samarspal utkik - installationer.
. Gratis att gå upp.

. Jag skulle gå dit oftare på kvällen.

– Lysprojektorerna för inte dra på mkt
energi...... LED.

– Ta med mig folk oftare.
Vattfärd!   . Sätta hammarby på kartan

globen
utkik – installationer.
kontors hus
bostadshus

Rediscovering energy in everyday life

In our previous and ongoing research, we have been exploring design as a means of visualizing energy in everyday life — mostly, however, this has taken place at the scale of product forms and interactions within the home and family life. In Ab|Norm, we took the opportunity to think further about relations between design and energy use — but on an urban scale and within civic life.

For two of the researchers, Ab|Norm is part of ongoing doctoral work in the fields of interaction and service design — therefore, it is one building block within a more extensive research framework. Thus, our focus has been on seeing how certain themes from previous projects might be deepened and expanded. It has been a testbed for thinking about if, and how, such themes might be extended to a larger spatial and temporal scale within the built environment and how our inquiry might be extended to another set of potential 'users' or stakeholders.

The starting point for the project was an active rediscovery of the city, taking the terms 'normal' or, conversely, 'abnormal' as lenses through which to view sites and situations. We made a series of excursions, documenting the presence of electricity sources, infrastructure and use. Alongside spotting potentials for energy efficiency and reduction, we also considered values such as security, ambiance, beauty, tradition, identity and conviviality. We took note of functions and forms that have become so ubiquitous that we may no longer even take notice — such as electrical boxes on streets and in parks, overhead wires crossing through public and private spaces, sources of street lighting and signage systems.

Documentation from these excursions provided information and inspiration for a series of analysis and ideation sessions back in our research studio. Discussing together, initial ideas began to emerge around themes — these ranged from ideas around what it might mean to embody or navigate statistics, to show off or make a show of energy use, and to exert energy to get energy. During these sessions, rapid and rough sketching began to function as a basis for communicating ideas and for developing design concepts. Sketches were manifested as hand-drawn illustrations and photo-montages — the point was not that the sketches were totally clear, original or attractive, but that they captured rather complex ideas and physically mapped out a set of concepts.

By externalizing and visualizing our ideas as sketches, we were able to discuss aspects of a theme or concept as well as to step back and take a larger discussion across the board. In internal sessions, as well as in a workshop with others from Switch!, a growing set of sketches provided a concrete basis for expressing a landscape of themes and concepts, at micro- and macro-levels, and for reconfiguring these by literally and physically rearranging the sketches as props during group discussions. As an extremely rough form of 'rapid prototyping', the sketches were easy to revise, evolve or discard, while still acting as placeholders for recalling ideas and discussions even if working sessions were days or weeks apart. The sketches became a sort of shared conceptual and concrete 'common ground'.

Having discovered from these working sessions how the sketches could function to frame and provoke a hands-on as well as high-level discussion around the themes and concepts depicted, we decided that the project would actually take the form of carefully selected concept sketches and of a workshop format within which the sketches would be used to engage a discussion with external stakeholders. We selected four sketches as a basis for further speculation on the concepts and issues at hand.

Interfering Statistics

This concept takes the form of large panels within a public plaza or park. The panels relate to different sources of local energy use, and they rotate to show real-time statistics about these. Interpretation and navigation is required to walk through — people must embody the statistics they create and decide whether to walk the path least taken or most well-trod.

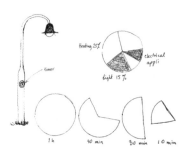

Lamp-Post Timer

This concept proposes interventions into public lighting systems. Basic functionality might include an on/off switch that provides a choice for illuminating a social gathering or dimming the light for a date; an advanced version might replace the bulb with a video projector to display real-time statistics about local energy use on the sidewalk in order to stimulate park debates.

Large-Scale Electricity Consumption Indicators
Lights on the facades of multiple apartment buildings make up a large-scale information display — signaling the energy consumption and trends in each individual building and enabling comparisons and competitions to be made between. The concept may simply network the lamps that are already commonly displayed on windowsills.

Public Hang- and Dry-Out
This is a physical structure installed in a neighborhood open space for locals to gather and hang out their laundry to dry. It's an energy-saving add-on to a laundromat and builds on the social aspect of doing laundry together — and makes a spectacle out of the sustainable and social aspects. Literally, it's about leaving one's (clean) laundry out to dry!

Staging a discussion with stakeholders

The four selected concept sketches were taken into a workshop as props for constructing a discussion with stakeholders in the energy and design sectors. Inspired by workshop techniques from participatory design, performative ethnography and game-based design methods, we planned and conducted a half-day workshop. Six participants were invited, including men and women of different ages and from disciplines including energy engineering, product and service design, art, architecture and landscape architecture. The workshop was designed to engage the participants both as 'users' of energy in their everyday lives as well as 'experts' with knowledge that might be brought to bear in other ways upon our project. Activities were sequenced in order to start from the first perspective.

To start off the workshop, the two workshop leaders gave a general and short presentation about the general research theme and, more precisely, the goal of the workshop. To get the participants more relaxed and acquainted, we played a game based on 'speed-dating', in which each person introduced themselves to another, then moved on to the next, until everyone had met one-on-one. After this, we met again as a group, and the workshop leaders gave an overview of the afternoon's activities and schedule.

The first activity was called 'An ordinary day in my life': "Think about a typical situation or happening in your everyday life that takes place in a public space. For example, it might be when you are taking your children to kindergarten, visiting a friend, or taking a long walk on a Sunday... Tell the story in three steps. What details are important in the story? Who is there? What does the environment look like? How do you feel?... Write down some key words and illustrate this through drawings or diagrams if you would like. The story should not focus

on energy and nor be work-related. The story does not
need to have a good ending or a punch line."

Individually, participants wrote and illustrated one
or more situations on their worksheets and, then, each
shared with the whole group. The intention behind this was
to invite a deeper personal engagement in the workshop
as well as to elicit meaningful stories with rich details
about social, material and emotional factors that could
be returned to later in the workshop.

For the next activity, the participants were divided
into three groups, which had been decided beforehand
to match up interesting competences and perspectives.
Each group was given a set of of four cards, each featuring
one of the concepts pre-selected for the workshop, along
with a new worksheet with instructions and space to
write and draw.

This activity was called 'An unusual day in my life':
"Choose two of the concepts that you think work best
within the situations that you described in the first activity.
Now, create two new stories combining the concepts
and the situations by asking yourselves 'Where is energy
present?'... Here are some things you might consider as
you make up the stories — How does the situation change
if the concept is intervened into it? How does it affect the
location and the people? Short-term, long-term? Positive
and negative aspects? What is interesting or exciting with
this concept? Where is it placed and why? How can the
concept be changed to fit into the setting? Is there a place
where it would fit better?... Draw a map or scenario of
where and how your story takes place. Document your
discussion on the worksheet."

The intention of this activity was not to generate
new concepts — as might be the goal of a co-design or
participatory design workshop — but to speculate on
what might emerge as the concepts were intervened into

an existing situation. In this case, it was important that the situations were familiar, personal and meaningful, providing a rich environment into which the concepts would pose potentially significant changes to how people might think, feel and act.

Indeed, the concepts themselves were deliberately provocative — introducing new modes of playful, political and social interactions. Rather than attempting to fully resolve the situation and the concept into a new or alternative design, a gap between the 'ordinary' (from the first activity) and 'unusual' (introduced in this activity) was intended to create another kind of discussion.

The workshop ended with a group discussion, in which the participants were asked to step into another role — that of their professional and disciplinary expertise — to discuss the concepts from this point of view.

Reflecting on the workshop afterwards, we noticed several aspects of the workshop design that proved effective. Starting the workshop by going deeply into participant's personal situations was a very good way to approach the idea of public space, which can often seem too abstract. Dividing the storytelling activity into three stages worked very well, since participants then had to reflect upon the details and events in their story — we ended up with elaborate and inspiring stories about Sunday strolls, meetings with friends in the city and daily commutes to work.

It was also important that the four concepts were not about being realistic and feasible — this allowed a sort of 'suspension of disbelief' and stimulated 'visions of the future' with the concepts. The second group, for example, adapted the concepts as they were inserted into the stories, leading to very interesting discussions about how they motivated their decisions. Their 'Public Hang- and Dry-Out' was placed in the south part of Haga park, which they thought was boring but closer to the city so that people didn't have to take the car (which would counteract the whole idea of saving energy).

While anchored in reality, participants were able to develop stories with rich details, personal meanings and diverse endings. In addition to valuable input for our own design and research development, fresh and interesting ideas also emerged.

We did find it difficult to focus attention on the social and political aspects — instead, design form and function tended to take over in participant responses. This may be due to many factors — such as the background of several from design-related fields. Further, our intention to create a gap between personal real-life situations and the ideas/ ideals reflected in the concepts proved difficult for the participants to grasp. For example, while one group placed all four concepts into one person's story, another group ended up focusing on details rather than the big picture, and the last created totally new concepts in order resolve their story.

To shift the emphasis in future workshops, we would like to experiment with methods of role-playing and model-making and perhaps activities in larger groups — while storytelling was effective as a device for engaging participants, perhaps writing and drawing limited spontaneous emotional responses and interpersonal dynamics.

An ordinary day in my life …

En vanlig dag i mitt liv...

Tänk på en typiskt vardaglig situation eller händelse i ditt vardagsliv som utspelar sig i offentlig miljö. Det kan t ex vara när du lämnar barn på dagis, besöker en vän eller söndagspromenaden. Försök återge denna händelse i tre steg, som en liten berättelse. Vilka detaljer är utmärkande för förloppet? Vilka är där? Vad händer runt omkring? Hur ser miljön ut? Vilken känsla bär du med dig? Skriv stödord och rita gärna!

Behöver beldsna centrum.

1 Promenad till Clas Olsson

Skall ökonkart - behöver timer för belysning -slå på/av för att inte tjuckar skall notera att vi är borta. Går med somen. Passerar APEA strömmen på torget. Vacker, återdomligmiljö. Möt okända människor, men bekanta miljöer

2 Besök på Clas Olsson

Letar timer i "djungeln". Diskutere rar interaktivitet med butikschefen - olika lösningar - remote interaction. Kanringa upp. Träffar oftast nåra bekanta. Känner flera i personalen - lite må nade - trevligt. Trivs i miljön, med massta bekanta pylar.

3 Promenad hem - möter Basmindsfamilj

Går hem - möter Bas mi med familj. De är från Indien och är nästan oigen känliga pga alla kläder de har på sig i kylan (runt 0°C), - vi tycker dagen är ganska skön. Samma miljö som i bild ett, men trevligt träffa bekanta och sina prata lite. förlöjer "behags känsla" att träffa bekanta

En vanlig dag i mitt liv...

Tänk på en typiskt vardaglig situation eller händelse i ditt vardagsliv som utspelar sig i offentlig miljö. Det kan t ex vara när du lämnar barn på dagis, besöker en vän eller söndagspromenaden. Försök återge denna händelse i tre steg, som en liten berättelse. Vilka detaljer är utmärkande för förloppet? Vilka är där? Vad händer runt omkring? Hur ser miljön ut? Vilken känsla bär du med dig? Skriv stödord och rita gärna!

1 APOTEK KONSUM / JERNET / VI / PARKERINGEN

Handla i didingö centrum ställer bilen på parkeringen - Försöker hitta parkeringsplats, irriterar mig på didngötorn. o surar - Massa folk är ute, barn säger går till klamresorn

2 SYSTEMBOLAGET

Börjar på systembolaget .... därefter Apotek, Systams, och Konsum eller Vi - Väljer mellan Konsum eller Vi lugn och ro på konsum men alltid slut på varor. Full fart på Vi men trångt och folk med babblisk bringner och Canada Grose jackor som pratar om seglingoch Åre.

3 FULL KUNDVAGN

- Slutar med överfull shoppin vagn - Urjobbigt att dra kundvagnen över parkeringen. Varför är de alltid så svåra att hörа! Särskilt när det är snö och slask. Lyfter in allt i bilen, kör hem.

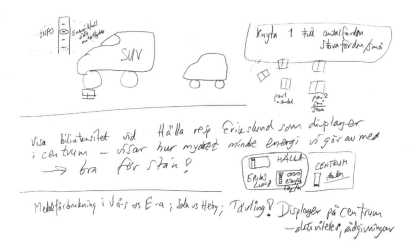

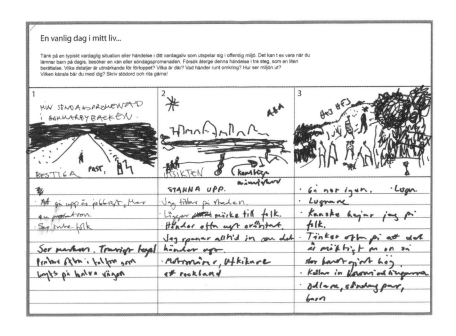

An unusual day in my life …

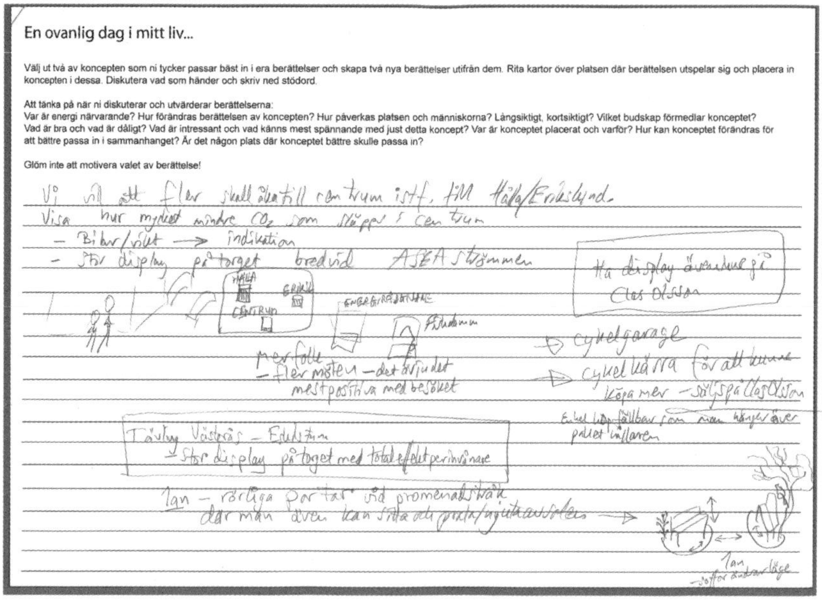

En ovanlig dag i mitt liv...

Välj ut två av koncepten som ni tycker passar bäst in i era berättelser och skapa två nya berättelser utifrån dem. Rita kartor över platsen där berättelsen utspelar sig och placera in koncepten i dessa. Diskutera vad som händer och skriv ned stödord.

Att tänka på när ni diskuterar och utvärderar berättelserna:
Var är energi närvarande? Hur förändras berättelsen av koncepten? Hur påverkas platsen och människorna? Långsiktigt, kortsiktigt? Vilket budskap förmedlar konceptet? Vad är bra och vad är dåligt? Vad är intressant och känns mest spännande med just detta koncept? Var är konceptet placerat och varför? Hur kan konceptet förändras för att bättre passa in i sammanhanget? Är det någon plats där konceptet bättre skulle passa in?

Glöm inte att motivera valet av berättelse!

(handwritten notes)

Vi vill att fler skall åka till centrum istf. till Hälla/Erikslund.
Visa hur mycket mindre CO$_2$ som släpps i centrum
- Bibir/vilet → indikation
- stor display på torget bredvid ASEA strömmen
  [Ha display även utanför på Clas Ohlson]

→ cykelgarage
→ cykel kärra för att kunna köpa mer - säljs på Clas Ohlson

mer folk
- fler röster - det ljudet
mest positiva med besöket

Tävling Västerås - Eskilstuna
Stor display på torget med total effektperinvånare

Tan - rörliga ... tar vid promenadstråk
där man även kan sitta och prata/inget arbete...

(second worksheet box — printed text)

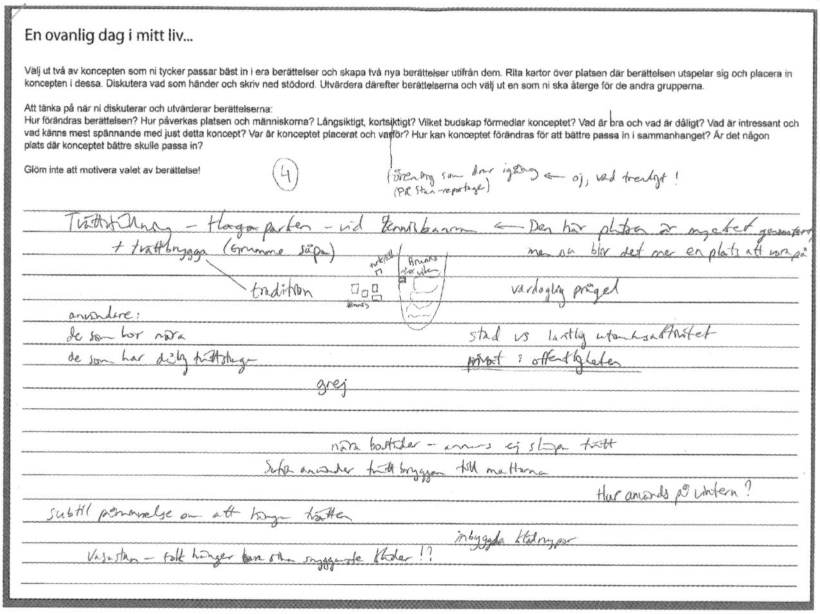

En ovanlig dag i mitt liv...

Välj ut två av koncepten som ni tycker passar bäst in i era berättelser och skapa två nya berättelser utifrån dem. Rita kartor över platsen där berättelsen utspelar sig och placera in koncepten i dessa. Utvärdera därefter berättelserna och välj ut en som ni ska återge för de andra grupperna.

Att tänka på när ni diskuterar och utvärderar berättelserna:
Hur förändras berättelsen? Hur påverkas platsen och människorna? Långsiktigt, kortsiktigt? Vilket budskap förmedlar konceptet? Vad är bra och vad är dåligt? Vad är intressant och vad känns mest spännande med just detta koncept? Var är konceptet placerat och varför? Hur kan konceptet förändras för att bättre passa in i sammanhanget? Är det någon plats där konceptet bättre skulle passa in?

Glöm inte att motivera valet av berättelse!

(4)   [berättelse som ... igång ← oj, vad trevligt!]
       (PR ... reportage)

Tvättstuga - Hagaparken - vid Svartån ← Den här platsen är ... genomfart
+ tvättbrygga (grönare tvätt)   men nu blir det mer en plats att vara på

tradition   vardaglig prägel

användare:
de som bor nära   städ vs tillfällig utanför aktivitet
de som har dålig tvättstuga   privat i offentligheten

grej

nära butiker - annars ej släpa tvätt
Soffa använder tvättbryggan till mattorna
                                   Hur används på vintern?
subtil påminnelse om att tvätta   inbyggda klädnypor

Västerstan - folk hänger bara ... engagerade kläder !?

En ovanlig dag i mitt liv...

Välj ut två av koncepten som ni tycker passar bäst in i era berättelser och skapa två nya berättelser utifrån dem. Rita kartor över platsen där berättelsen utspelar sig och placera in koncepten i dessa. Diskutera vad som händer och skriv ned stödord.

Att tänka på när ni diskuterar och utvärderar berättelserna:
Var är energi närvarande? Hur förändras berättelsen av konceptet? Hur påverkas platsen och människorna? Långsiktigt, kortsiktigt? Vilket budskap förmedlar konceptet? Vad är bra och vad är dåligt? Vad är intressant och vad känns mest spännande med just detta koncept? Var är konceptet placerat och varför? Hur kan konceptet förändras för att bättre passa in i sammanhanget? Är det någon plats där konceptet bättre skulle passa in?

Glöm inte att motivera valet av berättelsen!

① suv miljöbil

- Väg bilarna på parkeringen
  beliivande slunt, bilarna pumpar upp ett
  "moln" eller en rygs som blir större
- Belöna bilfritt handlande i varuror
  Visa bilintensitet på köpcentrum

③
Stor display/homtresh som jämför
el förbrukning i didigö a Nacka. didigö leder
sedan man infört hemlivning med elbil

Promenerar till centrum, i centrum är anhelganpet nästan fritt.
Parkeringen är halvtom och helvaemd, resten är cyhelparkerin. Kantresh (display) som visar in
bilarna har verkligen gett resultat. Jag går till torget, där visas model förbrukningen i didigö
och Nacha.
Jag handlar, fikar med en kompis, och ställer sedan alla påsarna i Hemlivring med elbil.
Promenerar hem i lugn och ro!

Speculating on consumption (ab)norms

Extending and further developing a set of themes in our ongoing research on visualizing energy, Ab|Norm speculates on the (ab/normal) forms of energy use in urban space and civic life. The project is manifested as a series of concept designs collected on cards, which constitutes both an archive of of our ideas relevant to this topic and a physical resource for engaging a wider discussion with stakeholders from, for example, creative and technical fields concerned with design and energy issues.

For us, the concept cards have functioned as conversation pieces or props for discussion — a conceptual stimulus and physical basis for discourse. To such ends, we have experimented with workshop methods for framing, sequencing and developing a discussion around the norms in current (and potential) strategies for designing and using energy in public space. An important aspect of our workshop was the inclusion of both personal and professional perspectives of participating stakeholders. From the workshop, we gained feedback upon our ongoing design research process and new ideas for future work. In particular, we see a range of ways for hard data and scientific statistics about energy to become present at different spatial and temporal scales in everyday life.

The concept cards, rather than design solutions or proposals, accompany a methodology for inquiring into norms embedded in various practices and among practitioners. Ab|Norm creates a platform for exploring relations between energy use in public and private space, between local and civic interests in energy use — and how such relations are structured by political forces, technical infrastructure, and by design.

In such terms, we also see the project as a platform for imagining alternative structures — for continuing to open up and ask questions...

Might 'Interfering Statistics' activate the public sphere in a local place? What effect might it have if we asked people to navigate energy statistics and choices as they navigate physically through a familiar place? Are there other ways in which we might connect personal acts (small steps) with political acts (social change)?

Un-hiding the hidden

"Remove" walls but keep the pipes inside so that they become more exposed and new design-elements. Pipes could be transparent. The veins of the building. Create social meeting place around these areas (tables, chairs...) One could also use warm water pipes as hand railings.

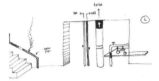

Interfering Statistics

Sliding door illustrating a horizontal bar diagram. The scale could be on the floor for example. The sliding door is in the middle creating two spaces on either side. These can be doors with variable widths. Two doors – two choices! The choices regulate the size of the openings.

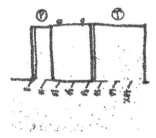

Choosing Side

One path for energy wasters, one for energy savers. You choose!

Interfering Statistics

Rotating gates – changes angle depending on live data like; heat consumption, number of cars in the parking garage, electricity use, time, temperature, ... The gates forces you to alter your path creating different paths depending on the current trends. Old walk paths slowly fade away as the grass grows.

Might the 'Large-Scale Indicators' effect self-perceptions and local interactions around energy through house-to-house comparisons? Are there other ways of 're-tuning' existing systems to better display the energy present? Are there other ways to think about statistics as a basis for locating energy choices where consumption takes place?

Energy Demands Energy

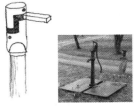

A tap that makes it harder to use hot water. Could be installed in public toilets or in an office.

One could also use manual water pumps that makes it harder to waste water.

Large Scale Energy Consumption Indicators

Possibly a set of taller buildings with visual indicators on the façade showing the current (and historical?) energy use of the building. People in the different houses can compare how they are doing compare to the others.

Each apartment could have a lamp placed in the window all facing the same direction. All the lamps would together work as a grid.

Interfering Statistics

Sliding bars that function as a transparent roof. The bars represent live data.

Could be more interfering as vertical walls.

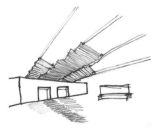

Energy Demands Energy

Energy should not be taken too easily. How can we think more about the equivalent labour that would be needed if we produced the energy ourselves? Re-evaluating the effort. How much are you prepared to work to get the energy?

An escalator that slows down the more people that uses it. Should you take the stairs or the slow escalator?

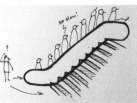

Might direct control via the 'Lamp-Post Timer' decrease light pollution or waste? How might such local choices facilitate more functions in the space or richer social interactions? How might security or privacy issues come into play? Are there further ways of thinking about the value(s) of local versus central control in public services?

Paved Way Sub Way

Carrying the new RFID-based community traffic card opens up shortcuts as a reward for your environmentally sustainable choices.

Example:
stones appearing in the water that you can jump on to get a shorter way.

Doors opening in wall

Energy Democracy Stickers

Make aware of energy elements in public space. Suggested movement with stickers that can be attached to lamp-poles, electricity boxes and such. Public space becomes a private issue. We are all responsible for our environments...

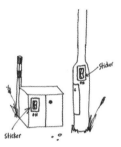

Lamp Post Timer

A timer switch that enables you to control when you need a light source. Create a personal social space where friends can meet and "hang out". The light spot could be a pie chart. Either as a count down (10min)
or as a pie chart illustrating different aspects of energy use, or environmental problems.

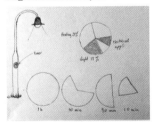

Making statistics becoming an integrated part in public space that can attract attention and create discussion. The decreasing pie-chart creates a symbolic connection between light (energy) and time conveying the fact that energy is a limited resource. It also emphasizes the idea of greater personal responsibility in public space.

Energy Demands Energy

A light-switch placed high up on a curved wall that requires physical effort to be used. That is, you have to put in your own energy to use "others". (The Physical Office!)

Might the 'Public Hang- and Dry-Out' attract social interactions in unexpected places around energy issues? Could such interactions lead to new forms of reflection on or interaction with energy afterwards? Are there other ways to think about the 'soft power' of local pride, gossip and flirtation as a basis for rethinking energy use?

Reinterpreting the electricity box

These boxes are everywhere but they have become so integrated and common that you rarely think about them. The purpose of the discrete shell is to attract little or no attention. It's only function. What we don't see, we cannot criticize.

One could try to acknowledge their existence by adding new functions. Maybe there could be small tables where you could sit with your friends and drink tea... Only after people have rediscovered these boxes they can have an opinion.

What happens when you offer someone the opportunity to sit down and integrate with these boxes? Is the electricity becoming more tangible? If so, is it exciting or frightening? Are you surprised that they are everywhere? Are they really a natural part of the public space?

Slowly Changing Norms

Light is slowly getting darker then suddenly going back to its highest value.

Energy politics

Installation outside the Parliament. Borrow aesthetic language from the voting board inside Plenissalen to show the energy consumption of the parliament. Focusing on the politicians is an interesting way of putting focus on an important issue. Who is the most energy conservative- do they act as they preach?

Public hang- and dry out

A chance to meet outside as an alternative to the Laundromats common in some parts of the world. A chance to meet new people and do the environment a favour at the same time. Challenge the norm of only meeting people in bars, cafés and over Internet.

Ab|Norm is part of Switch!, a design research program at the Interactive Institute sponsored by the Swedish Energy Agency.

Project team Loove Broms, Karin Ehrnberger, Ramia Mazé, with thanks to Brendon Clark. A special thanks to all the workshop participants.

Symbiots

Jenny Bergström, Ramia Mazé,
Johan Redström, Anna Vallgårda
with Olivia Jeczmyk and Bildinstitutet

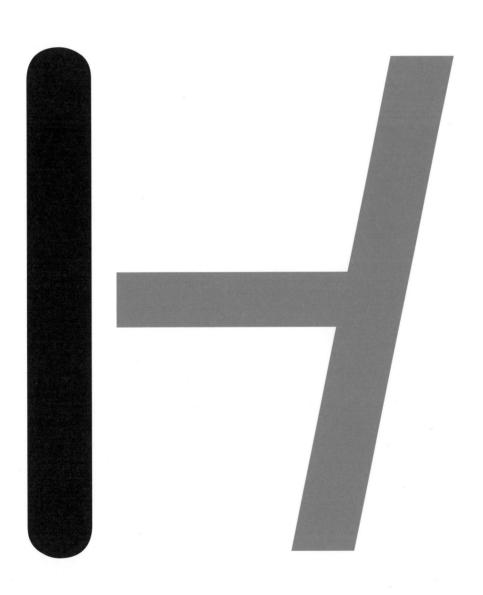

'Symbiots' imagines forms in the urban landscape that operate parasitically — emerging and thriving when households or neighborhoods reduce energy consumption. For people, the provision of these as public functions acts as a reward. For Symbiots, it lures people away from their private habitats and energy-consuming habits, thus leaving more power for others in the electricity grid. The project queries increasing competition for natural resources and current human- (versus eco-) centered design paradigms. Symbiots takes the form of a photo series in the genre of contemporary hyperreal art photography. Produced as posters, these have been the basis for raising awareness and discussions with neighborhood residents.

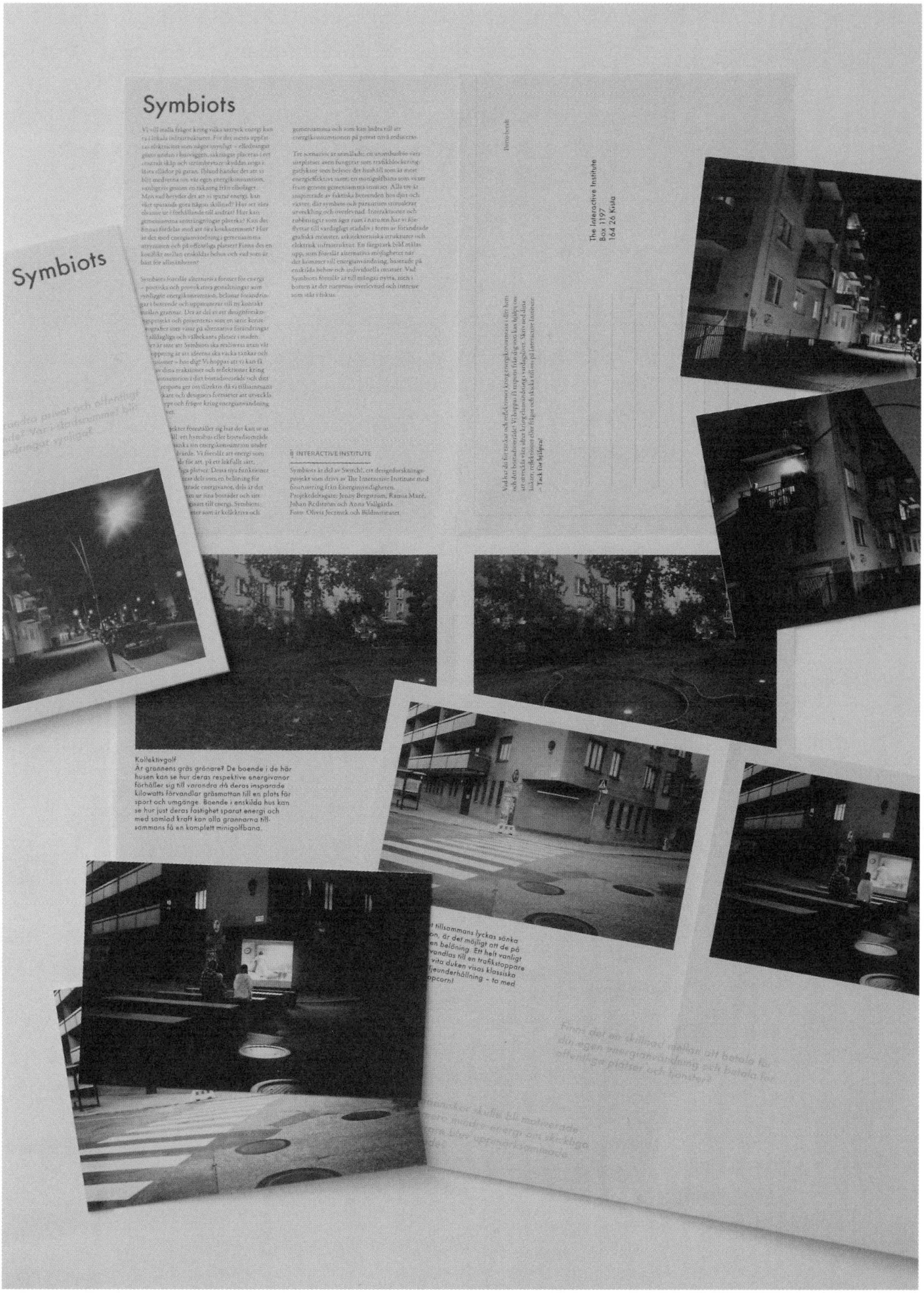

Symbiots

Symbiots

Kollektivgolf

§ INTERACTIVE INSTITUTE

The Interactive Institute
Box 1197
164 26 Kista

Intervening into energy systems

Within Switch!, we were interested in how variables in existing value systems can be shifted or rebalanced. For example — how the introduction of an unusual or extreme behavior in public space causes a reflection upon or change in others' behaviors. Or, how the introduction of a new thing at home changes perceptions of other pre-existing things. We explored how design interventions (as things or happenings) into these systems might shift the existing values, not only exposing habits, norms and standards, but also effecting a rebalancing or renegotiation among actors/variables.

In this project, we started by speculating on energy in the city: In what forms is energy production/delivery/sale/use visible? How would exposing interactions around energy or intervening new mechanisms transform the situation? What alternative interests might be served? How might other sites and actors become focal points or 'power'-stations within a locality? How would this transform the cityscape, in space and over time?

Considering the city as a sort of ecosystem, we imagined negotiations that might take place among diverse organisms and interests in the case of limited resources. We began to speculate on issues of competition and collaboration within a limited energy system — how these might be manifested in interactions among participating actors and in the material forms and technical logics that govern such interactions. Exploitation and theft, for example, raise issues of who owns what, and how resources are distributed, appropriated and consumed. Benefits and rewards raise issues related to persuasion, peer pressure and social contract.

We looked to notions of *symbiosis* to think further about ecosystemic interactions. In biology and botany, symbiosis characterizes relationships within 'the living together of unlike organisms', including pathologies of harm/benefit ranging among the mutualistic, parasitic and commensal. We also looked to cultural theory, in which parasitism applies to practices of sharing and stealing electricity in nomadic settlements and developing countries. Related issues of (political) power are raised in tactical media, in which the term applies to strategies for usurping the power of hegemonic media, economic and political systems.

As a brief, symbiosis operated as a conceptual framework for examining (inter)dependencies within a system, including pathologies and power negotiated among human and non-human actors.

Having thus set a sort of brief, we began to develop the design space, focusing on electricity consumption within a system comprising diverse actors and agencies. Rather than stand-alone forms or autonomous functions, we considered interventions into existing infrastructures and systems, and the temporal as well as spatial aspects of interactions. In relation to 'energy ecologies in everyday life', Symbiots developed as an investigation into the complexity of human- and eco-systemic interactions around energy consumption instantiated in mundane situations and local sites.

To explore how symbiotic interactions might play out in actual situations and sites — and in relation to existing functions such as shopping, partying, playing and eating — concept development unfolded through conceptual mapping, local site-seeking and sketching.

Symbiots

Sketching conceptual interventions

Early concepts explored parasitic forms of reactions to high/low energy consumption in local contexts. Each explores different sets of motives and actors, as well as various formal manifestations and functional behaviors.

We took concept and design development 'in the field'. Over several days, we explored different neighborhoods in Stockholm, seeking particular sites that could be interesting to situate concepts. Along with unique or well-known areas in the city, we also explored popular and commonplace spots in terms of types of inhabitants and visitors, amenities and activities, reputation and composition. The process of concept-mapping, site-seeking, and sketching interventions was iterative. Over several days spent in our studio and around town, we developed different sketches and gathered to discuss initial concepts, sites found and new concepts generated or elaborated in response.

To locate concepts within existing neighborhoods, as well as to test out different ways that they might appear or communicate visually, sketches took the form of montages on top of the photos taken when out and about in the city. The 'Square parasite', for example, was manifested in different sites — the landmark tourist destination of Sergels Torg in the center of the city, in a cosy semi-public courtyard habituated by families and in a square ringed with popular cafes for young professionals — using the same formal/functional mechanism.

Different locations exposed differences in who might be effected, how and why. For example, the 'Crossing parasite' in a suburb suggested a potential clash between old-timers and outsiders but, in a progressive part of town, suggested impromptu social gatherings and shared child-minding among young families. Around these sketches, we were able to transform the discussion from one about the design features and urban functions to potential social conditions and consequences.

Square parasite

The Square parasite lives underneath a square. It expands and shifts to rearrange the surface of the square, creating a 3D landscape from the 2D surface. This landscape can function for activities — as an arena for performers and spectators or as outdoor furniture for local stores and neighborhood gatherings.

Light parasite

Like the Square parasite, this parasite rearranges surface patterns. In this case, cracks in the ground form contours and game features for mini-golf. This can be built up as a single hole or an entire putt-putt course, with more or less extreme ground conditions to reflect the inhabitants of nearby apartments or buildings.

Playground parasite

The parasite has discovered that children are the key to the human heart. Thus, it takes on the form of playground equipment — for example, it takes on the form of a swing by rising up and assembling itself from a pile of 'junk', just like the masts of a mini-ship are raised in the classic souvenir bottle.

Crossing parasite

The parasite has taken the form of a crosswalk. As it thrives at night or on good days, each stripe rises to the height of a bench, thus creating a row of benches. This furnishes a space for activities – the benches can be used for an outdoor cinema projected on the facade of a nearby building. It also brings traffic to a stop, forcing people in cars to park and walk.

Transparent parasite

The parasite has discovered that humans appreciate beautiful things. It takes on the shape of art works, colored rocks, fish ponds, poetic engravings or small gardens. These are revealed, in response to neighborhood conditions, by illuminating a vitrine sunk within a pavement or square so that its contents are put on display.

Facade parasite

The parasite travels from window to window across the facade of a local block of flats. It is stocked with colorful lights, outdoor furniture, barbeque equipment and even a TV-satellite dish. Highlighting a certain flat, the balcony arrives to provide instant (though temporary) decoration, display and entertainment functions.

Symbiots

Materializing concepts

Three concepts were selected to develop further as scenarios. Sketching had revealed the complexity of factors within each site as well as multiple issues that we wanted to raise within a nuanced discussion around energy consumption. Choosing three allowed us to develop complex depictions within each as well as a range of other possible spaces and times, social and cultural manifestations.

We chose photography both as a communication medium to convey complex and nuanced messages as well as a prototyping platform for 'implementing' design concepts that were not possible (or even desirable) to build. Indeed, the challenges of building them at a full scale and in any realistic technical or aesthetic version would have reduced the set of issues that we could have raised and directed attention away from the complexity of factors to a selection of a few factors that might feasibly have been prototyped in another way.

After considering different genres of photography, including those more prevalent in architecture and journalism, we turned to fine art photography and developed a collaboration with a professional photographer and an institute specializing in 3D-rendering.

We began a series of photoshoots, carefully staging the composition of actors and objects, lighting and material qualities. Subtle alterations to the texture and color of light, for example, resulted in dramatic differences in how attention was directed in the picture and the mood conveyed — the color green could be dark and sinister or bright and suburban. Subtle articulations to objects and surfaces gave rather dramatic visual cues about the potential for 2- or 3D transformations of the built environment that has otherwise become so mundane that such patterns have become invisible. These were carefully crafted within the photoshoots and in post-production.

In Symbiots, we imagine a parasite that lives off energy from the local electricity grid. It thrives when there is low demand on the system, when it has a chance at competing for resources. During a phase of low energy consumption within a neighborhood, and thus reduced competition, the parasite surfaces within the urban landscape as it consumes energy from the grid. Since revealing itself involves the risks involved with being noticed, the parasite has chosen a symbiotic strategy, shaping itself into forms and functions that are pleasing to inhabitants of the neighborhood.

Suddenly and sometimes spectacularly visible, these serve to lure people out of their private habitats and away from their energy-consuming habits, thus further reducing private energy use. A successful instance of this parasite would create an addictive relationship with the local inhabitants, who would become dependent on the forms and it provides — a less successful one, however, could potentially die off. Survival depends upon its ability to minimize the energy consumption of local residents sharing the resources of the host grid.

Staging local conversations

The photo series presents particular and provocative concept of energy consumption, instantiated as scenarios represented and located within specific sites. The photos produced and scenarios depicted can be seen as a sort of constructed and physical manifesto, a set of ideas specified, situated and materialized. We have intended these to be a basis for making ideas — and questions — operational towards potential and future stakeholders. Toward this end, we have considered the photos as interventions within two different contexts: a (future) exhibition within a museum or gallery, and; a local conversation with neighborhood residents.

We returned to Aspudden, a neighborhood in which one of the photoshoots took place, with a poster designed to present the project and the photos. Intended, in this case, as 'conversation pieces', the fine art refinements of the photographs were downplayed. Two photos were printed as glossy snapshots, intended as mementos, with a written invitation to post them on the family refrigerator. Posters were distributed to all the apartments in buildings within a particular block in Aspudden, and interviews were conducted by two of the project team with five households.

The posters and photos framed conversations opening onto many related issues. For example, only the kitchen light is on when we arrive to meet Britt. She tells us that she thinks a lot about energy savings — "We just have one planet". Upstairs, Sven is on a municipal committee concerned with energy, but he treasures the heated bathroom floor and always leaves a light on for the cat. Across the way, Mikael is concerned that families with small children are disadvantaged by energy-savings policies. Olof has environmental ideals but cynically believes that individual and business interests will win out.

Issues of individualism, collaboration and competition within the local environment emerged. Responses articulated significant social and even political issues around energy use, posited within reflections on their own personal, family and communal situation.

In a variety of ways, these conversations explored values related to everyday interactions with energy. Grounding articulations of general opinions or larger issues, the strangely familiar photos seemed to stimulate the expression of rich stories, personal beliefs, local politics and existing relationships. Besides our in-person conversations, we foresee further related interactions among inhabitants after our visit. Indeed, we discovered that our repeated visits — for site-seeking, photo-shooting and interviewing — had already sparked local discussions around the topics raised. For us, this suggested a potential for Symbiots to operate not only as a critical practice, but as a critical *social design* practice.

Interview with Britt (87-years old) who lives alone in a 3-room flat. When we met, she had just come back from a haircut and her weekly swim.

When she cooks and bakes, Britt saves energy. Yesterday she made four cakes at once, so that she didn't have to heat up the oven again and again. When she cooks, she turns the hob off once she thinks it will be cooked enough with the afterheat. She saves energy both because of the economy and the environment —

"Vi har bara en jord / We just have one planet."

Discussing the Public Spotlight, she volunteers that she would like to have more light on the balcony:

"Well, I'm disappointed that I didn't think about that when I had the electrician here, to get a socket so I could have a lamp (on the balcony). And since I have to pay for it myself (the installation), things that don't belong to the building, it gets expensive."

"But why didn't I arrange so I could have outdoor lighting?"

Who's responsibility is it to save energy?

"I think it's our own responsibility. We have to feel that responsibility, I think. The housing cooperative can't go around and turn off lights for everyone."

When we leave, she tells us,

"I can spread the word to the others around here..."
"We often meet and discuss things."

We knock on the door and Olof answers. It's his girlfriend's flat, with original interior design details and vintage furniture. As it turns out, the first floor apartment doesn't have a balcony! The flat is dark, Olof has been in the kitchen.

About saving energy...

> "In general, on a societal level, a lot of electricity is used by private actors, businesses and public facilities."

> "Consumption on an individual level doesn't really matter when it comes to environmental issues — it's more factors that are beyond individual control."

Who's responsibility is it?

> "There has to be some movement both on the authority level and then some awareness at the individual level. One could give as many reasons as you can imagine for why you should consume less."

About Public Spotlight...

> "I don't really know, it depends. People tend to be pretty individualistic, and it's becoming more and more like that, so it would probably work on some level."

> "Well, competition is popular."

Interview with Olof (23-years old), who is staying over in his girlfriend's flat — when we talk to him, he is just about to cook dinner for when she comes home from work.

Interview with Sven (73-years old), who lives
with his wife and Benny (a cat). He recognizes
us from Britt's description of the events around
our photo-shoot during the previous weeks.

We are welcomed into a neat flat with cosy corners and small lights throughout. Sven and his wife are pleased with their electric stove and heated bathroom floor, which is on all the time. They have low-energy bulbs but, since they are not happy with the light, the bulbs are placed where not much light is needed.

Do you know how much energy your neighbors consume?

> "There was this guy on the top floor, but he's not in the building anymore, he had some machine going, you could hear that he was doing something. But, other than that, it's just normal people here."

About Public Spotlight, he repeats...

> "Det var ju roligt / That's neat."

How do you think about your own energy consumption?

> "We are aware on a daily basis of the environment, but it's not like a special thought or effort like 'we must sort our garbage'."

> "I keep the light on when we are out of the house — for Benny."

As we leave, Sven mentions,

> "Then [Britt] will soon come by, knock on my door, and say that these girls were here again."

Symbiots

Mikael and Mia both come and open the door for us. They are a bit hesitant, but invite us in. Their apartment is very cosy, with a lot of toys and books around, and not really anywhere to sit. We start by introducing the project and the Public Spotlight concept —

About the Public Spotlight concept:

> "I can imagine that when you come home at night after work, you will surely look for the lamp to see where it is. The risk is that there is always a small, one-person household that consumes very little electricity in comparison to those of us with two children, it's a lot of cooking and there's a washing machine..."

What about energy that is shared or common in the building?

> "When you know that you can save money on it, then you save energy, but you would not do it for everyone. That's how egotistic people are... For example, if you have to tumble-dry something, and you go downstairs, you may put on the machine for fifty minutes even if you know it may only take thirty, just to make sure that it will be dry without having to go back and forth."

Can people think differently about their own consumption?

> "When you can save money, when you get your own bill, then I think that people care more. I think so. That's how egoistic we are. In general, at least."

Who's responsibility is it?

> "There has to be demands or pressure from the authorities... It helps with promotion by the state."

Interview with Mikael (29-years old) and Mia (4), who are watching children's TV and waiting for Mia's mom and little brother to come home from a friend's house.

We might tend to think of energy as a matter of technological infrastructure or a system of economy and regulation, but we need only look to its local manifestations in our own backyards to understand that political power, social contracts and human costs are at stake. Nor are technical terms separate from those of ethics and aesthetics. Symbiots is an example of how an inquiry might be crafted and staged through alternative 'cultural imaginaries'. With symbiosis as a point of departure, scenarios of interaction around energy depict varieties of dependency within non/human relations.

Symbiots depicts three scenarios: 'Street Cinema' — an event that arises as a traffic-stopping experience for locals; 'Public Spotlight' — street lights that spotlight household energy efficiency, and; 'Competitive Golf' — a mini-golf course that builds up through collective effort.

These scenarios have been elaborated within Symbiots to investigate social and cultural aspects of interactions with common resources such as energy. Each secenario is portrayed in two states, to emphasize how, where and why a site or situation look different in relation to changing patterns in energy consumption. While we imagine that Competitive Golf might come to life at the end of the working day, the Street Cinema would need a more sustained and collective effort — thus, each operates in relation to different temporal cycles and trends in energy use, patterns of public/private life and rhythms of urban routines.

The scenarios deal with different scales of energy behavior. Public Spotlight emphasizes the presence of an individual occupant within the semi-public community of an apartment building and also the general public of the streetscape; Competitive Golf operates on the basis of household-to-household competition between house-proud neighbors who own property in an affluent part of town, and; Street Cinema creates a collective public space for residents (blocking outsiders) in a mixed-use neighborhood. Competitive Golf operates through peer-to-peer competition, Public Spotlight promotes individualism within a collective and Street Cinema relies on collaboration for a common good.

Each deals with complex issues of public and private, spotlighting private citizens in the public eye (and the perhaps double-edged celebrity of being singled-out), the semi-public space of courtyards and balconies (infringed upon, in Competitive Golf, by teenage trespassers), the common neighborhood space of the street crossing within the wider urban traffic infrastructure (in which access to both private and public access is temporarily blocked). Energy consumption is thus placed in a social context, raising complex issues around private life and public rights, relations between consumption, habitation and citizenship, relations between social competition, collaboration and ex/inclusion.

Each situation has been selected and the photograph crafted to articulate a particular position in relation (and contrast) to the others. Instead of simply reducing energy consumption to a question of reward and punishment, the nuances and implications of the different situations depicted in the photos are intended to draw out a rich engagement and imagination on behalf of the viewer about the more complex nature of 'good' consumption and 'model' society.

Such multiplicity of ideas and implications are gradually exposed as one looks at a photo from afar versus up close, and as the photos are arranged in relation to one another.

Switch!

Street Cinema

If everyone in the area works together to lower energy consumption, a reward may be in store at the end of the week. An ordinary street crossing transforms into traffic-stopping event. On show are classic nature and family films — bring your own popcorn!

Public Spotlight

Street lights serve the public good — and, in this instance, private citizens. These lamps shed light on the apartment with the best energy habits within reach. Balconies suddenly come to life for new activities — and as a stage for models of good behavior.

Competitive Golf

Who's grass is greener? These neighbors can tell how their energy behaviors match up — their savings manifests as a sporting activity on their own doorstep. Individual houses can distinguish themselves and collective action can build up a whole golf course.

Symbiots is part of Switch!, a design research program at the Interactive Institute sponsored by the Swedish Energy Agency.

Project team Jenny Bergström, Ramia Mazé, Johan Redström, Anna Vallgårda. Photography by Olivia Jeczmyk and Bildinstitutet.

Thanks to Karin Ehrnberger and family, Aude Messager, Thomas Thwaites and Basar Önal for participating in the photshoots. A special thanks to the neighborhood residents of Aspudden, Kungsholmen and Skanstull.

Further reading A version of this text was previously and originally published as Jenny Bergström, Ramia Mazé, Johan Redström and Anna Vallgårda, "Symbiots: Conceptual interventions into energy systems," in *Proceedings of Engaging Artifacts* (Oslo: Nordic Design Research Society, 2009).

Explanation

Ramia Mazé, Johan Redström

Design and research

Design is often said to be about 'value creation', referring to the power of design to effect meaningful and valuable experiences for consumers as well as material and brand value for clients and stakeholders. Operating on behalf of producers, design is bound into larger projects of increasing economic and symbolic capital. With respect to consumption, design is no longer, if it has ever been, solely about satisfying the basic human needs of an individual or society, but also about creating needs and even manufacturing desire.[1]

Historically, this persuasive power of design has been employed in the service of expanding consumption. Indeed, design came into being at a particular stage in the history of capitalism, along with the scales of economy presumed by industrialized mass production and mass-market consumption. Disciplines such as industrial and interaction design have grown up around interest in expanding the market and profitability of the emerging electric and electronics sectors.

Given this history, as well as contemporary awareness of certain undesirable ecological side-effects of previous modes of production and consumption, perhaps it is no wonder that design has often been seen as part of the problem within the environmental discourse. In response, diverse strategies are collecting under the general umbrella of 'sustainable design'. Much effort has been directed at improving existing manufacturing systems, increasing the energy efficiency of processes and products, and promoting green consumption. Others move away from production of and desire for the 'new', towards the endurance, reuse and sustainment of existing things or continuing and closed systems of production.[2] Indeed, some are reconsidering the material basis of design altogether, evident in increasing interest in service and experience design, and the application of design to the

Note — A version of this text was previously and originally published as Ramia Mazé and Johan Redström, "Switch! Energy Ecologies in Everyday Life," *International Journal of Design* 2, no. 3 (2008): 55–70.

1 — See Adrian Forty, *Objects of Desire* (New York: Pantheon, 1986).

2 — For example see Jonathan Chapman, *Emotionally Durable Design* (London: Earthscan, 2005); William McDonough, *Cradle to Cradle* (New York: Northpoint Press, 2002); Peter-Paul Verbeek and Petran Kockelkoren, "The Things that Matter," *Design Issues* 13, no. 3 (1998): 28–42; Tony Fry, "The Voice of Sustainment," *Design Philosophy Papers* 1: www.desphilosophy.com/dpp/dpp_index.html (accessed online October 30, 2008).

business and politics of sustainable development.[3] On the defensive, much has been done to reposition design as part of the solution.

However, it is not simply a matter of being part of the problem or part of the solution — the current situation cannot be reduced to such terms. Due to the complexity involved in sustainability, it is simply very hard to consider and negotiate all aspects necessary to achieve a fail-safe solution, particularly since such solutions must somehow be compatible with the current state of affairs. Given the difficulty of foreseeing the future consequences of design decisions, it is possible that things we regard as solutions here and now may produce further problems elsewhere in the world or later on. Humanitarian and environmental interests intersect and even compete within sustainable design, pointing to larger historical and philosophical tensions between ideas of nature and culture, progress and change, individualism and collectivism. Within this complex set of interests and ideologies, causes and effects as well as problems and solutions become difficult to identify, much less to address head on.

3 — For example, see: Arnold Tukker and Ursula Tischner, eds., *New Business for Old Europe: Product-service development, competitiveness and sustainability* (Sheffield, UK: Greenleaf, 2006); Ezio Manzini and François Jégou, *Sustainable Everyday* (Milan: Edizioni Ambiente, 2003); Bruce Mau and Jennifer Leonard, *Massive Change* (London: Phaidon, 2004).

Explanation

Critical practice

Design can be characterized by its particular capacity to negotiate complexity. Rather than problems that are definable, objective and consensual, which may characterize some of the problems treated within the natural sciences, design deals with social and political problems that can never be finally or universally solved. This entails that (sustainable) design cannot only be concerned with problem-solving, as its task is often formulated within the tradition of technical rationality. Indeed, design problems might be understood as an open set of issues with many possible resolutions, the design process as reflexive inquiry in which new questions or even problems may be generated along the way, and the product of design as one proposition among many and competing ideas.[4]

Within design, modes of reflective and critical practice engage with such problematics. For the reflective practitioner, each move within a design process is the basis for self-reflexive and wider analysis that is allowed to reframe or redirect the whole.[5] Conceptual and critical design reflect upon the conditions and processes of design — but, moving beyond describing and exposing these, practitioners also actively engage in posing new questions and problem frames. As Jane Rendell articulates:

> Projects that put forward questions as the central tenet of the research, instead of, or as well as solving or resolving problems, tend to produce objects that critically rethink the parameters of the problem itself.[6]

Tendencies toward critical practice are explicitly concerned with problem-finding in disciplinary discourse and wider society, with an ambition to open up a practical and tangible arena for criticism from within, and as, design.[7]

4 — See Horst Rittel and Melvin Webber, "Dilemmas in a General Theory," *Policy Sciences* 4 (1973): 155–169. See also Richard Buchanan, "Rhetoric, Humanism, and Design" in *Discovering Design*, Richard Buchanan and Victor Margolin, eds. (Chicago: University of Chicago Press, 1995), 23–68.

5 — Donald Schön, *The Reflective Practitioner* (New York: Basic Books, 1983).

6 — Jane Rendell, "Architectural Research and Disciplinarity," *Architectural Research Quarterly* 8, no. 2 (2004): 145.

7 — Ramia Mazé and Johan Redström, "Difficult Forms," *Research Design Journal* 1, no. 1 (2009): 28–39.

Such tendencies are not unprecedented — heritage might be traced through the modernist avant-garde, anti-design since the 1960s and critical architecture.[8]

For example, anti-design contested design blindly 'in service' to values set by historical convention or hegemonic ideologies, espousing a political and ethical agenda proper to design — "Otherwise we will end up by designing beautiful electric chairs or mountains of rubbish,"[9] as Superstudio proclaimed. These historical examples, and a growing number of contemporary practices, attempt to diversify or counter mainstream views on what design is and what it should be about.[10] Relating to critical and social theory from other disciplines, critical practitioners engage in (de)constructing the intellectual and ideological foundations proper to design, thus reconfiguring how we might think about the agency and responsibility of design.[11]

In addition to this conceptual agenda, such tendencies also expand the practical means and methods for making forceful propositions. Alternative forms of professional practice and collaboration across disciplinary borders have been a basis for reworking existing conditions, situations or institutions of design, and alternative processes and products have been a basis for critiquing conventional modes of production and consumption. For some, this has meant resistance to traditional imperatives of mass production or market consumption. For example, 'paper architecture' applies the persuasive visual narratives and tangible forms of design, but it is primarily produced for publication and exhibition rather than for construction and inhabitation.[12] Controversial propositions made through alternative channels for (ideological) production have succeeded in constructing a very public and sometimes more participatory discussion around societal issues.

8 — See Ramia Mazé, *Occupying Time* (Stockholm: Axl Books, 2007); Magnus Ericson and Ramia Mazé, eds., *DESIGN ACT: Socially and politically engaged design today* (Berlin: Sternberg / Iaspis, 2010).

9 — Quoted in Peter Lang and William Menking, eds., *Superstudio* (Milan: Skira Editore, 2003), 120.

10 — For further examples see Andrew Blauvelt, ed., *Strangely Familiar* (Minneapolis, MN: Walker Art Center, 2003); Anthony Dunne and Fiona Raby, *Design Noir* (Basel: Birkhäuser and August Media, 2001).

11— See Jane Rendell, Jonathan Hill and Murray Fraser, eds., *Critical Architecture* (London: Black Dog, 2007).

12 — For example see Magnus Ericson et al, eds., *Iaspis Forum on Design and Critical Practice — The Reader* (Berlin: Sternberg, 2009); Catherine de Zegher and Mark Wigley, eds., *The Activist Drawing* (Cambridge, MA: MIT Press, 2001); Neil Spiller, *Visionary Architecture* (London: Thames & Hudson, 2006).

Research through (critical) practice

In terms of design research, this might be seen in relation to 'research through practice', or practice-based research.[13] Central to both critical practice and practice-based research is consideration of design as a mode of knowledge production — the objects produced act as a "material thesis", embodying certain intellectual and ideological arguments. As Alex Seago and Anthony Dunne articulate:

> The object itself becomes a physical critique... research is interpreted as 'conceptual medeling' involving a critique of existing approaches to production/consumption communicated through highly considered artifacts.[14]

Or, it may be seen as a sort of design criticism — though critical practice moves beyond analysis and interpretation. Indeed, its effects in material form and on behavioral transformation is what differentiates design — as a material practice — from the hermeneutic practices of criticism or 'research into design' that typically take place in a humanities or social science context.[15]

Research through (critical) practice opens for new ways of thinking and doing design today. Design imagination, skill and craft can be applied to stage a debate on pressing issues that might otherwise be difficult — even undesirable — to realize in other forms. Designers engage not only in solving or resolving problems but also in questioning how problems are set, by whom and why. This is an alternative approach to the emerging challenges to design — indeed, if we only respond in a reactive, defensive or pragmatic mode, we might unwittingly affirm the conserving mechanisms of convention or become complicit with the values of other systems and institutions.

13 — See Christopher Frayling, "Research in Art and Design," *Royal College of Art Research Papers* 1, no. 1 (1993–1994): 1–5.

14 — Alex Seago and Anthony Dunne, "New Methodologies in Art and Design Research," *Design Issues* 15, no. 2 (1999): 16–17.

15 — For example compare: Frayling "Research"; Stan Allen, "Practice vs Project," *Praxis* 0 (1999): 112–123. See also Mazé, *Occupying*.

Further, this opens a new space for design research to engage with larger discourses within the sciences and humanities. In addition to its strategic and practical forms, and building upon its history of ethical and political concerns, research through (critical) practice might also expand how we reflect and act upon environmental issues in design.[16] Indeed, as the ideas and strategies around sustainability proliferate in contemporary design, we must not only develop solutions but intellectual and ideological foundations for reflecting critically on alternatives. Indeed, we must recognize the social construction of the sustainability discourse itself.

16 — Ramia Mazé, "Criticality Meets Sustainability," in *Proceedings of Changing the Change* (Turin, Italy: Politecnico di Milano and Politecnico di Torino, 2008).

Explanation

Everyday energy ecologies

Engaging with ideas within environmental discourse and sustainable design means, to some extent, engaging with the complexity of causes and effects, emerging problems and preexisting 'solutions', material and human factors. This implies that it is not only the subject of design (its intellectual and ideological concerns or objectives) that must be considered — but also the object(s) of design.

Design has, in fact, long moved past a narrow focus on the form of discrete objects, demonstrated by increasing interest in product-service systems, consumer/user experiences and lifestyle values.[17] In such terms, we may think of the object of design not as a discrete and self-contained artifact, but as made up of and bound into a more complex set of relations. There are a number of attempts to articulate this in terms of 'ecology' within design discourse — for example, 'information ecologies', 'service ecologies' and 'product ecologies'.[18]

Traditionally, the term 'ecology' has been applied within the natural sciences to describe the complexity of relations among living organisms and their physical surroundings. Multidisciplinary variations upon the subject include 'cultural ecology', which takes an anthropological, political and geographic view upon the relations between cultures and their natural resources and material conditions.[19] Current discussions around 'political ecology' deal not only with how political, economic and cultural factors relate to nature, but the social construction of the environmental discourse itself.[20] In this line of thinking, knowledge about the environment is understood to be mediated by the instruments, interpretations, concerns and protocols of the sciences and other disciplines — including the arts, which have significantly influenced socio-cultural conceptions of nature.[21]

17 — For examples and discussion see Johan Redström, "Towards User Design?" *Design Studies* 27, no. 2 (2006): 123–139.

18 — For example see Bonnie Nardi and Vicki O'Day, *Information Ecologies* (Cambridge, MA: MIT Press, 1999); "Services" in *Designing Interactions*, Bill Moggridge, ed. (Cambridge, MA: MIT Press, 2006); Jodi Forlizzi, "The Product Ecology," *International Journal of Design* 2, no. 1 (2008): 11–20.

19 — For example see James Gibson, *The Ecological Approach to Visual Perception* (Boston: Houghton Mifflen, 1979); Mark Sutton and E.N. Anderson, *An Introduction to Cultural Ecology* (Oxford: Berg, 2004).

20 — See Paul Robbins, *Political Ecology* (Cambridge, MA: Blackwell, 2004); Bruno Latour, *Politics of Nature* (Boston, MA: Harvard University Press, 2004).

21 — See Max Andrews, ed., *Land, Art* (London: RSA/Arts Council, 2006); Ian Simmons, *Interpreting Nature* (New York: Routledge, 1993).

Richard Peet and Michael Watts articulate:

> The environment itself is an active construction
> of the imagination, and the discourses themselves
> assume regional forms that are, as it were,
> thematically organized by natural contexts. In
> other words, there is not an imaginary made in
> some separate 'social' realm, but an environmental
> imaginary, or rather whole complexes of imaginaries,
> with which people think, discuss, and contend threats
> to their livelihoods.[22]

Instead of focusing on the separation of living and non-living systems, or even human and non-human actors, political ecology treats these as a hybrid blend of social perceptions and biophysical experiences that cannot be known or described in any absolute or final way. Bruno Latour argues that the systems constituting humans and their environments intersect, overlap and co-determine one another.[23] Thus, current studies of relations between ecology and society treat, as Carl Folke and Lance Gunderson put it:

> Humanity and nature as co-evolving systems
> that interact within the bounds of the biosphere
> at various temporal and spatial scales and
> across scales.[24]

Any thing is inevitably located within, and constituted by, these interconnected and interpenetrating systems, generating effects that are local and locatable, at points of intersection or interaction.

Contemporary thinking in material culture and the sociology of technology places design in relation to material and political ecologies. On one hand, designed

22 — Richard Peet and Michael Watts, eds., *Liberation Ecologies* (London: Routledge, 1996), 37.

23 — See Latour, *Politics*.

24 — Carl Folke and Lance Gunderson, "A Kaleidoscope of Change," *Conservation Ecology* 6, no. 1: www.ecologyandsociety.org/vol6/iss2/art19 (accessed online October 30, 2008).

things are understood to be comprised not only of basic matter but to embody the actions and intentions of their makers and commissioners.[25] As crossovers of social and natural elements, things can be described both in terms of immanent dynamics of matter-energy and in terms of structured power and morals.[26] Enabling certain actions and disabling others, things have an agency in prescribing aspects of their subsequent reception and future use.[27] On the other hand, it is people who buy, adapt and use things appropriated for their own purposes within personal practices and cultures of use.[28] Indeed, product consumption includes not only integration of given affordances and embedded scripts, but the emergence of alternative interpretations and programs of use.

Designed things, thus, might be understood as a site of evolving and emergent interactions among human and non-human actors, material and political forces, technical and social processes. Focus shifts from the traditional spatial object(s) of design to the interactions within, around and through many things within a particular setting.

This has consequences for thinking about sustainability. For example, it may not be feasible to center design around the present and future of one solution or proposal, as if we might project from the current state of a particular product to a more efficient, eco-friendly or otherwise preferred future version of the same. To the extent that interactions emerge in the space between the things that people assemble and adapt to their own values and purposes, these cannot be designed nor even anticipated by design. In this sense, sustainability is not something that can be embodied in the object(s) of design but that must emerge from within the complex ecologies constituting everyday life.

It also suggests another potential for design as an intervention into everyday ecologies. Consider the effect

25 — Bruno Latour, *Pandora's Hope* (Cambridge, MA: Harvard University Press, 1999).

26 — For example, Jane Bennett, "The Force of Things," *Political Theory* 32, no. 3 (2004): 347–372; Thomas Dant, *Materiality and Society* (New York: Open University Press, 2005); Elizabeth Grosz, ed., *Becomings* (Ithaca, NY: Cornell University Press, 1999).

27 — Madeleine Akrich, "The De-Scription of Technological Objects," in *Shaping Technology/Building Society*, Wiebe Bijker and John Law, eds. (Cambridge, MA: MIT Press, 1992), 205–224.

28 — See Elizabeth Shove, *Comfort, Cleanliness and Convenience* (Oxford: Berg, 2003); Jack Ingram, Elizabeth Shove and Matthew Watson, "Products and Practices," *Design Issues* 23, no. 2 (2007): 3–16.

of introducing, for example, a new piece of clothing or furniture into a wardrobe or household — not only does it add something 'new', it changes the perception of previously existing things as the 'old'.[29] We might compare this with the approach of brand development — while a consumer's lifestyle, values and habits cannot be designed in totality from above, they can certainly be influenced from the bottom up. While branding might typically try to change perceptions in order to encourage people to replace their old things with more of the new, we might also think of intervening things that prompt reflection on other values. This opens up for ways of working with systemic change from the bottom up, in terms of design form and forms of use, rather than top-down systems design.

Consider another example: relations to energy in everyday ecologies. This cannot only be constituted by the infrastructures of electricity production and distribution nor the electric and electronic devices depending on these infrastructures — but also by regimes of value, purpose and habit held by people in a social and cultural context. Indeed, electricity raises a further interesting issue. Other technologies and products may have a more obvious novelty value, objectified and packaged in ways that more forcefully intervene into the new. However, the structures, objects and actors participating in electricity use — such as grids and infrastructures, plugs and appliances, producers and consumers — are already deeply integrated into the everyday and extensively covered within sustainable development. In fact, the question of energy is perhaps less a matter of introducing something than of rediscovering it, of uncovering something currently hidden and taken for granted. So, here, we might take another look at when and where design interventions might matter.

29 — See David McCracken, *Culture and Consumption* (Bloomington: Indiana University Press, 1990).

Switch!

Much of our research inquires into how design can promote awareness of energy use in everyday life.[30] In our previous 'Static!' program, for example, we focused on the relation between products and their users and redesigned the repeat and daily interactions with products in ways that would invite reflection not only on, but in and through, energy use.[31] 'Domestication' studies of several of the artifacts, placed in households for extended periods of time, revealed how such interactions were embedded in more complex arrangements of furnishing and devices in the home, perceptions of light and nature during different seasons, and ongoing communications and negotiations within daily family life.[32] In response, we became interested in expanding our focus beyond the proximate scale of real-time interactions between an individual user and a discrete product, a typical scope for research and practice in industrial and interaction design.

Inspired by contemporary thinking in material culture and sociology of technology, Switch! considers design as an intervention into multiple and interpenetrating technical, material and social systems — or ecologies. Here, we attempt to shift from isolated people-product interactions to consider the larger spatial scale and longer-term aspects involved in architectural and urban interactions. Taking into account an expanded notion of site and situation, we also consider more elements involved in staging and inviting participation into sustained interactions. This involves the aesthetics of material forms — as well as the aesthetics of a larger experience and longer narrative in which forms are embedded. We attempt to make visible and tangible the connection of energy use to wide and ongoing issues affecting the locality, community and society. Thus, the focus shifts from energy, and even electricity *per se*, to the ecologies it provides for.

30 — See Mazé, "Criticality."

31 — Ramia Mazé, ed., *Static! Designing for Energy Awareness* (Stockholm: Arvinius Förlag, 2010).

32 — Sara Routarinne and Johan Redström, "Domestication as Design Intervention," in *Proceedings of Design Inquiries* (Stockholm, Sweden: Nordic Design Research Society, 2007).

In order to influence perceptions and values around energy use, we have been investigating the place and potential agency of design within the multiplicity of actions and accumulated interactions in complex social and urban situations. In addition to the design of materials, objects and interfaces, design is also engaged to tell persuasive narratives and to stage experiences and debates. The design of interventions and the use of design methods become a platform for exposing existing habits and hidden norms as well as for proposing alternative actions and views. These propositions have been developed through practical experimentation, the materialization of design examples and the extension of these into debate forums, participatory workshops and field studies.

This shift from products, to the relations within product ecologies that new designs might expose and transform, is not only a consequence of our own research, but also a response to significant developments in the field. Between the conclusion of Static! in 2005 and now, a range of products that are in some ways similar to the design examples we developed have entered the marketplace (including a few of our own). Besides this perhaps double-edged success of encouraging production and consumption, there are also conceptual reasons driving us to push the boundaries further. This is not innovation for innovation's sake — but it is about the creation of a reflective or critical relation to practice that requires a certain tension between 'what is' and 'what if', between the possible or probable and the challenging or speculative 'imaginaries' needed to deepen and develop a discourse.

Research structure and participants

Design research in the area of sustainability can be approached in any number of ways. This implies that a particular research program needs to frame a more specific set of theories — as 'critical practice' and 'energy ecologies' have within Switch!. Interdisciplinary research also requires a boundary around a substantial common ground for diverse participants to relate and work within. Participants in this program, for example, came from art, design, anthropology, architecture, philosophy, computer science and engineering, each bringing a different set of concerns, methods and expertise. The danger of interdisciplinary research is that it becomes more of a meeting place for conversation than a deep collaboration. As a sort of 'provisional knowledge regime',[33] a research program, its frames and boundaries, enables participants to engage in design experiments and exploring consequences of various theories and practices through joint work together. As such, it is also instrumental for challenging and re-negotiating relations among the many disciplines involved, thus facilitating a genuinely collaborative effort.

The first phase of Switch! was guided by a series of collaborative sessions spanning one or two days. Each session focused on different aspects of the overall program, such as concepts of ecology in design, design materials and experimentation, participatory design and design ethnography, explored through presentations, readings, collaborative analysis, hands-on workshops, critiques and joint writing. This established a common conceptual and practical background for the participants. In the course of events, certain ideas persisted and collected around the intersection of complementary research questions, areas of interest and expertise within smaller groups of participants. These were further positioned in relation to topics in sustainable design and articulated as a series of

33 — See Thomas Binder and Johan Redström, "Exemplary Design Research," in *Proceedings of Wonderground* (Lisbon, Portugal: Design Research Society, 2006).

potential design research briefs. Elaborated not only in terms of the core ideas, but also methods and feasibility, collaborators and stakeholders, several of these briefs were taken forward by project teams as starting points for experiments.

It has been our intention that the research management of the program act as a sort of curation. Rather then a more traditional approach, which might involve top-down organization of teamwork, comprehensive project planning, assignments and briefs set in advance, the main structuring devices here are the programmatic ideas and initial collaborative sessions, as well as ongoing critiques, seminars and writing. More specific ideas, methods, and design concepts were developed locally and over time, within smaller teams and through experimentation. We have worked with such open-ended formats before,[34] but Switch! has involved a particular assembly of participants involved in other activities in parallel and outside this program, including long-term doctoral studies, other research and teaching work and commercial consultancy. Much needed to be left open for evolution along the way on the basis of agendas formed through individual initiative and teamwork.

34 — For example, Johan Redström, Maria Redström and Ramia Mazé, eds., *IT+Textiles* (Helsinki, Finland: Edita / IT Press, 2005).

Design examples and experiments

Within the overall program, it is a series of experiments within smaller teams and resulting design examples that constitute the main bulk of the research. During the first phase of Switch!, certain concepts grew and persisted, and became the basis for further experimental work defined and carried out within smaller teams — evolving into 'Energy Futures',[35] '3Ecologies',[36] 'Green Memes',[37] 'Telltale',[38] 'Ab|Norm'[39] and 'Symbiots'.[40] Each drives the program through more specific and deeper inquiry into the themes and questions set out in the program. However, just as theory and practice do not necessarily meet in any direct, absolute, or even equivalent relation in practice-based research,[41] experiments do not operate as a proof or test of the program but to learn about, reflect upon and challenge certain general or pre-conceptions. Within each, specific working methods are developed as well as concepts elaborated through one or more visual and tangible artifacts.

The ambition was not to develop a single or optimal design, but to create a repertoire of examples for raising and discussing certain ideas among participants in Switch! as well as among other stakeholders and with the public. We also targeted professional and research communities, within the design, energy and public sectors, through research papers and presentations, personal interviews and field studies, participatory workshops and experimental performances. The diverse nature of the processes and concepts entails that the design examples cannot relate to the general theoretical issues on a direct or one-to-one basis, nor that they exhaust the space of possible design responses to the program. Indeed, there are many ideas left open to further investigation — rather than 'problem-solving', this kind of research through (critical) practice might well end by raising further questions and possibilities.

35 — See p.5
36 — See p.45
37 — See p.81
38 — See p.101
39 — See p.133
40 — See p.159
41 — See Mazé, *Occupying*.

Switch! is an attempt to create a space for reflecting upon the current status and strategies within design discourse concerning sustainability and environmentalism. In order to provoke critical reflection, rather than popular appeal and commercial incitement, we have attempted to create a distance from commercial product development. It has not been our intention to create a new set of solutions, or potential products, but to open a space between established and alternative values. Indeed, it seems necessary to complicate the problem/solution rhetoric around sustainable design, since dialectics and reductionism may not help us come to terms with the scale of the current challenges and the complexity of issues at hand. Thus, our ambition is not to converge upon a single problem or solution, nor a roadmap to a particular preferred future, but to materialize a territory of possible viewpoints as a basis for curating — and catalyzing — a conversation in the here and now.

To evade a growing genre of design one-liners and shock tactics that verge on 'climate porn', we have also described here our development of a more substantial historical and theoretical basis for framing our approach to critical practice, including relations to critical social and political theories around ecological issues in other fields. Steering clear of both greenwashing and eco-horror, future utopias and dystopias, we have been attempting to get at a more fundamental set of issues within design. While refusing both simplistic and extreme reactions, we might instead locate more specific, subtle and constructive strategies for engaging with the complexity of the current design problematics. In this, we believe that design research has a possibility to act as a sort of curation in the development of a mature debate about environmental issues by materializing diverse — and perhaps even conflicting — values in forms and formats that people can relate to and participate in.

In response to certain problematics within contemporary (sustainable) design, we have been rethinking the object(s) of design research and practice. For one thing, we attempt to circumvent the conventional preoccupation of design critique and history with discrete design objects, which often reduces design discourse to questions of form and function, usability and marketability. In light of current environmental issues, we attempt to expand consideration of the values that design might affect by drawing attention to the larger ecologies of systems, relations and interactions that objects are located within. This does not mean that we abandon questions of form and function — indeed, research through (critical) practice acknowledges the power of aesthetics and materiality as well as the persuasive and performative potentials of objects — but these are means for redirecting attention to other ends. The design examples, thus, are clearly locatable within architectural, interior, product, graphic and interaction design, but are motivated by and directed at exposing an alternative set of issues.

While the materiality, craft and aesthetics of design objects doubtless effect subsequent reception, we might ask further questions about how these effects might relate to intentions such as stimulating 'reflective use' or 'design for debate'. Indeed, given the power of a new object to propagate something beyond its own appearance, to locate a material point of intersection or interaction within multiple ecologies, we might also want to inquire into particular situations in order to understand an intervention at work. This might involve designers directly in an 'art of staging' within a site or situation, or design methods considered in terms of a sort of 'experimental anthropology'.[42] In some examples (Telltale), the objects produced are intervened into real households to evaluate aspects of performance and perception of the object in use,

42 — See Isabelle Stengers, "The Cosmopolitan Proposal," in *Making Things Public*, Bruno Latour and Peter Weibel, eds. (Cambridge, MA: MIT Press, 2005), 994–1003; Latour, *Politics*. See also Joachim Halse and Brendon Clark, "Design Rituals and Performative Ethnography," in *Proceedings of Ethnographic Praxis and Industry* (Copenhagen, Denmark: American Anthropological Association, 2008).

while others (Symbiots, Ab|Norm, and Energy Futures) experiment with alternative formats for scenario planning, design ethnography and experience prototyping in order to debate norms and imagine alternatives.

Further, we might consider the potential objectives — together with the object(s) — of design research in relating to environmental problematics. Cultural and political ecology argue that ideas about nature and sustainability are socially constructed — which introduces the possibility of making conceptual or discursive interventions that de- and re-construct such ideas in order to open up for alternative valuations and views. This might take a departure in the reframing of 'imaginaries', with some potential relation to the 'visions of the future' and 'alternative nows' that have been topics in critical practice (Symbiots and Energy Futures). Another might be the instruments and mechanisms through which we measure and value the environment — through, for example, alternative data sets, future predictions, consumer reports and categories of valuation (3Ecologies, Telltale and Green Memes).

In addition to the objects produced, the aesthetics of techniques for visualizing, storytelling, performing and debating have discursive dimensions. We wanted to encourage more nuanced or thoughtful responses to a potential object, so as to counteract tendencies towards commonplace responses of "I want this, where can I buy it?" or, correspondingly, "I do not like this — I'm not going to buy it!". Therefore, many of the design examples have a rather unsettling or ambivalent character, which was achieved through exploring and testing out different aesthetic strategies. For example, substantial attention was given to a material intervention responding to multiple direct and historical inputs for expressing change in terms of aging and resiliance (Telltale), to the complexity and contradiction of everyday anthro- versus eco-centrism (Symbiots), and a mixed assemblage of extreme futures and a strangely familiar present (Energy Futures).

The Switch! design examples are not meant to shock nor solve — their purpose is to propose and map out a set of new ways of thinking that throw the 'old' into sharp relief. By populating the design space with more options and alternatives, our intention is to elicit a tension between the actual and the potential, thereby undermining our habit of silently assuming the already established. It is not meaningful to evaluate such alternatives on the basis of whether they are better or worse than what exists already — they are not intended to be placed alongside others in an already rather crowded product market — but to articulate competing ideas within a larger discourse. Nor are conventional terms for creating or assessing value, such as utility, usability or appeal, ends in themselves, but means for opening up speculation on other ends altogether.

As recent debates around environmentalism demonstrate, approaches to environmental problems are inevitably tied to ideological and normative positions that must be continually examined and debated. We need only look at traditional conceptions of nature as resources quantified in terms of 'use value' and 'exchange value' — such terms have long governed how related problems are set, with profound consequences for the premises and limits of conservation initiatives and environmental policy.

Within current environmental thinking, there are fresh calls for design participation — and not only for problem-solving. When Isabelle Stengers characterizes design as "an art of staging", she also poses what we might take as a brief for critical practice:

> How can we present a proposal intended not to say what is, or what ought to be, but to provoke thought, a proposal that requires no other verification than the way in which it is able to 'slow down' reasoning and create an opportunity to arouse a slightly different awareness of the problems and situations mobilizing us?[43]

Sustainable design must incorporate mechanisms for critically reflecting on the role and responsibility of design in shaping human experience and changing social conditions. Rather than attempting to preserve the *status quo* or return to a previous state of affairs, this requires acknowledging the productive and persuasive power of design in creating the 'new'. Besides new solutions (or problems), this can include the formation of reflective practitioners and alternative ideas. As an art of staging, design might meet sustainability in 'problem-finding' — opening environmental problematics to an expanded range of values and stakeholders.

43 — Stengers, "Cosmopolitan," 994.

About Switch!

This book is part of Switch! — a design research program at the Interactive Institute sponsored by the Swedish Energy Agency (Energimyndigheten) in 2008–2010. The Interactive Institute Swedish ICT is a research institute that conducts applied research and innovation through creative and participatory processes.

Additional support was received for developing design examples through: the Smart Textiles Initiative, led by the Swedish School of Textiles at the University College of Borås and funded by the Swedish Governmental Agency for Innovation Systems (VINNOVA); Forms of Sustainability, a project at the Interactive Institute funded by the Swedish Research Council (Vetenskapsrådet).

Participants in Switch! received additional support through individual artistic grants, research projects and doctoral studies at other institutions including: Martin Avila through the School of Design and Crafts at the University of Gothenburg, Sweden; Jenny Bergström through Konstfack University College of Arts, Crafts and Design, Sweden; Loove Broms through Linköping University, Sweden; John Carpenter through Iaspis / Swedish Arts Grants Committee (Konstnärsnämnden); Anna Vallgårda through the IT University of Copenhagen, Denmark.

Switch! has also been part of educational curricula at: Umeå Institute of Design, Sweden, through the 'Design Ethnography and Participatory Design' course led by Brendon Clark, Ramia Mazé and Camille Moussette within the Interaction Design MA program, and; Konstfack University College of Arts, Crafts and Design, through the role of Ramia Mazé on the faculty of the Experience Design MA program and the 'Research Through Practice' MA course.

Martin Avila (SE/AR) is a designer, consultant and a lecturer in industrial design at Konstfack University College of Arts, Crafts and Design in Stockholm.

Jenny Bergström (SE/DE) has a background in textile design, and she works as a designer, researcher and educator in Stockholm and Berlin.

Loove Broms (SE) is an interaction designer currently pursuing a doctorate at the KTH Royal Institute of Technology in Stockholm.

John Carpenter (US) is an interactive digital artist, design consultant and educator in California.

Brendon Clark (SE/US) is a senior researcher at the Interactive Institute in Stockholm specializing in design anthropology, innovation and participatory design.

Karin Ehrnberger (SE) is an industrial designer currently pursuing a doctorate at the KTH Royal Institute of Technology in Stockholm.

Alberto Frigo (SE/IT) is a lecturer and researcher specializing in artistic approaches to ubiquitous computing and social media.

Ramia Mazé (SE/US/FR) is a senior researcher at the Interactive Institute specializing in critical and participatory methods within sustainable design and social innovation.

Medium (SE/UK) is a creative studio based in Stockholm producing projects related to public space, architecture and visual culture.

Aude Messager (FR) is an industrial designer specializing in anticipation methods for user-centered and service design.

Johan Redström (SE) is a professor of design at the Umeå Institute of Design at Umeå University in Sweden and formerly design director at the Interactive Institute.

Thomas Thwaites (UK) is a designer working with speculative projects involving technology, science and futures research.

Anna Vallgårda (DK) is an assistant professor at the IT University of Copenhagen, where she specializes in 'expressional' interaction design.

Basar Önal (SE/TR) is an experience and communications designer with a specialization in participatory and futures methods.

maoworks (UK) is a design agency that recently became Spotspot. Tobi Schneidler, Tom Ballhatchet and Solon Sasson participated in Switch!

Olivia Jeczmyk (SE) is a professional photographer who collaborated with Bildinstitutet for her work in Switch!

Book editor and Switch! leader Ramia Mazé

Switch! book contributors Martin Avila, Jenny Bergström,
Loove Broms, John Carpenter, Brendon Clark, Karin Ehrnberger,
Alberto Frigo, Ramia Mazé, Aude Messager, Johan Redström,
Thomas Thwaites, Anna Vallgårda, Basar Önal, maoworks
(Tobi Schneidler, Tom Ballhatchet and Solon Sasson),
Olivia Jeczmyk and Bildinstitutet.

Acknowledgements We are grateful to Sara Backlund and
Christina Öhman for their contributions to the Switch! program
and to Björn Tillman at Printografen.

Publication concept and design Martin Frostner and
Lisa Olausson at Medium.

Photography Project teams (unless otherwise noted)

Printed by Printografen AB, Halmstad, Sweden

ISBN 978-91-980924-0-0

Publisher Interactive Institute Swedish ICT,
Box 1197, SE-164 26 Kista, Sweden, info@tii.se